THE DAY THE CHICKEN CACKLED

Reflections on a Life in Pakistan

*For Ann Swain,
God bless you!*

*Bettie Rose Addleton
2010*

Bettie Rose Addleton

CROSSBOOKS
PUBLISHING

CrossBooks™
1663 Liberty Drive
Bloomington, IN 47403
www.crossbooks.com
Phone: 1-866-879-0502

*The cover photograph depicts the author, her husband, and son embarking for Pakistan
in 1956. The background design is from an **ajrak**, a block printed textile common in the
Sindh Province.*

Cover designed by: David Orr

First published by CrossBooks 12/08/2009

ISBN: 978-1-6150-7087-9 (sc)
ISBN: 978-1-6150-7107-4 (hc)

Library Congress of Control Number: 2009941231

Printed in the United States of America
Bloomington, Indiana

This book is printed on acid-free paper.

"The past and the present are walking now together.
They are singing a hymn."

-- David Bottoms

"For I know the plans I have for you, declares the Lord,
plans to prosper you and not to harm you,
plans to give you hope and a future."

-- Jeremiah 29:11

For my grandchildren

John, Adriana, Alexandra, Iain, Cameron and Catriona

and for my beloved husband, Hubert

who shared this journey with me

ACKNOWLEDGMENTS

How can one fully acknowledge the immeasurable generosity including time, love, patience, instruction, criticism, friendship, and encouragement given to me during the writing of this book?

Two organizations, WorldVenture and the International Mission Board (SBC), exercised faith in allowing us to serve for 34 years in Pakistan. Without colleagues and nationals I would not have this story to tell. They were and remain an indelible force in my life. They number in the hundreds and it is impossible to name each one.

Friends, acquaintances, and strangers have all urged me to write about my experiences in Pakistan. Collecting journals, letters, and photos has been time consuming. Finding time and a quiet place in a busy household was a challenge. My husband Hu supported my efforts with his willingness to eat whatever I had time to prepare for us. Many times he prepared the lunches. And always the breakfasts!

My three children--David, Jonathan and Nancy--may have been skeptical in the beginning but as the project continued they offered their enthusiasm and encouragement. My daughter-in-law Fiona and son-in-law Jeff have been quietly supportive.

Six wonderful grandchildren--Adriana, Alexandra, Iain, Cameron, Catriona and John–have all known of my determination to write this manuscript, showing interest and respect for "grandma's book." It is primarily for them that I have taken it to completion. I want them to know more about the background and legacy that we are passing on to them. Hopefully, it will also help them to better understand their parents and themselves, cherishing who they are and where they have come from.

I would be remiss if I failed to acknowledge Jonathan's willingness to read and reread the manuscript, offering constructive criticism balanced with encouragement and affirmation. During his occasional "home leaves," he gave graciously of his time and energy to help push this project toward completion. He also sorted through boxes of photos, helping to organize them for my selection. Thank you, Jonathan.

Clare and Sandy Camp set up my laptop, taught me how to use it, and provided tech support all the way. David Wall of Wall Digital

Media and Paige Sires with Smith & Watson, Inc. emerged just at the right time with their professional skills.

Ms. Isabel Wright, a writer herself, ignited the spark that fired me into action. Dr. Ben Griffith, former head of the English department at Mercer University, told me that I had a story to tell. Until now neither of you were aware that you sent me on my way. Dr. Mary Wilder, author and retired English professor at Mercer University, read the manuscript in its earliest form and returned it with encouragement, assuring me that some day it would appear in book form. Kitty Matheny, bless her heart, never gave up urging me to write my story.

None of these friends are held accountable for mistakes or errors. I am totally responsible.

PREFACE

From the moment I arrived in Pakistan in May 1956, I knew I was in a strange world, unlike any that I had ever seen or experienced. There was vibrancy and energy about what was then a new country, one that had become independent less than a decade before. There was genuine optimism as well. Pakistan, in 1947, had been carved out of British India to become a new nation with a majority Muslim population. In the view of its leaders, it was only a matter of time before it would emerge as a model Islamic state, setting an example for the rest of the world to follow.

I was privileged to live in Pakistan for more than thirty years, experiencing first hand the growth as well as the tragedies and disappointments of a country that now often figures in the international news. In those years, too, there were times when the wider world became aware of what was happening in Pakistan. These events included wars with India, natural disasters, the rise and fall of military governments, and the emergence of East Pakistan as the independent nation of Bangladesh. More recently, events have also included violence, terrorist attacks, wars in Afghanistan, and the rise of a militant Islam with an impact far beyond the borders of Pakistan.

While witnessing the rise of this more militant variety of Islam in Pakistan, I also saw the slow fading of what had once been a strong colonial past. Gradually, many of the names that the British had given to towns, streets, and buildings in Pakistan disappeared, replaced by more Pakistani ones. Colonial cemeteries that had once been carefully maintained and reflected the tragedies of the colonial past became overgrown, the inscriptions faded, and the headstones sometimes falling apart. Gradually, too, some of the more organized aspects of British rule–an efficient railway system, a local administration dominated by elite civil servants, courts that somehow seemed to work–became only a dim memory.

Alongside changes going on in Pakistan, I also observed the tremendous changes that took place in the United States during those years. As a child growing up in rural Georgia, there was no Pakistan on the map at all. It was simply part of a massive pink area demarcating the British Empire. I had never met a Muslim, seen a mosque, or heard the call to prayer. Now, having retired to Middle Georgia where I was born and raised, my grandchildren play soccer near a large new temple built by Hindu emigrants from India. Both Hindus and Muslims have become part of the Middle Georgia community. The first African-American mayor of the city where I live was a Muslim.

When we arrived in Pakistan, the population of the entire country was less than forty million; now, it is the world's sixth largest nation with a population exceeding 170 million. Then, the country was largely agricultural and rural; now it is a nuclear power with one of the most rapidly growing urban populations in the world. Then, many Americans couldn't find Pakistan on a map; now, it often features in newspaper accounts and on television news shows. Everyone can identify Pakistan.

Having lived for many years in Pakistan, I have no illusions about the challenges the country faces or some of the forces of violence unleashed in recent years. Books have been and are being written chronicling current affairs and the historic events now underway. At the same time, Pakistan is for me much more than a newspaper headline or a comment on television. I know the flesh and blood that lies behind the headlines. I know what it is like to live in a country that seemingly exists at the edge of a precipice all the time. The social milieu in which I lived hardly ever figures in the news and rarely emerges from behind the shadows of the historical accounts.

In retrospect, some of the most ordinary aspects of life turn out to be the most fascinating and ultimately revealing. Many of the years I lived in Pakistan were spent in a quiet and seemingly remote part of the country. Later I moved to Pakistan's largest city, with a population greater than that of many countries. What once seemed strange became common place. What once seemed different took on all the features of normalcy. In reflecting on my life in Pakistan, I am most interested in sharing some of the ordinary and every day experiences. All have been colorful, sometimes humorous, and always memorable.

I always felt that my ultimate calling was one of creating a home and family in the midst of all the history-making events swirling around. My husband's work was demanding of him and the family. It was not easy to create a home that offered peace, tranquility, stability and an oasis not only for us but also for our colleagues and neighbors. Therefore, my reflections come neither from history-making events nor the missionary aspect of my and my husband's work. Rather I have chosen to dwell on the ordinary and what some may consider mundane. However, for me these years have been extraordinary and anything but mundane.

Visitors to provincial towns in Pakistan often remark at how few women can be seen walking the streets. Those who venture out are almost always covered from head to toe in a *burka*. This fact alone makes it even more remarkable that I, a Western woman with all the freedoms implied, lived for more than three decades in Pakistan. I never wore the *burka*. However, I did wear the *shalwar/khameez* and *duputta*, a very modest, stylish and immensely comfortable dress. Pakistan today continues its custom of segregation on the basis of gender. However, one must acknowledge that powerful and influential women have emerged in Pakistan and South Asia, assuming both national and international prominence.

Over the decades, my own encounters with Pakistan centered on women who lived in a gender-segregated world. They admired and appreciated my attempt in learning their language and adapting to their customs. By and large, they were open, hospitable, caring, honest, and very patient in teaching me the complex as well as the common areas of their lives. I could not have lived among them for so many years without their loving and lasting friendship.

While enjoying and appreciating their confidences, I also realize how private most of them were as it related to outsiders. Privacy was and is an issue. To honor that privacy, I have chosen to substitute other names for their real names and sometimes I do not use names at all.

I also need to emphasize that the following narratives are based entirely on my memory and experience. Others may remember events differently. Though some facts might have become obscured in my memory, the very essence of my story remains and is imprinted in all that I am. These are my memories and experiences as I have lived them and remember them.

It is not an easy task to condense a lifetime into a few dozen pages or a few thousand words. In reality, a life well-lived cannot be contained within the bounds of a single book cover; even a library cannot fully capture it. However, what I have tried to do in the Chapters that follow is to recount and reflect on some of the more astonishing and amazing people I have encountered, relationships I have enjoyed, and experiences I have had during the many years in which I lived in the Islamic Republic of Pakistan.

Map of Pakistan

TABLE OF CONTENTS

Chapter One

GETTING THERE

Our long journey from Middle Georgia to Pakistan started on April 3, 1956 in Macon, Georgia. A crowd of well-wishers–friends, relatives, church members–were already waiting at the airport to see Hubert (hereafter called Hu), our seventeen-month-old son, David, and me depart. I was very excited. This would be my first plane flight. I had never been far from home except for a trip with a cousin to Washington, D.C. following my high school graduation some eight years earlier. However, Hu and I had spent 6 weeks in Canada for Linguistics study.

After hugs, kisses, tears, and a final prayer, we boarded the small propeller plane for the first leg of the journey that would take us to Pakistan. It took less than an hour to reach Atlanta where we changed to a larger plane bound for Newark, New Jersey. Disembarking, our hearts pounding with nervous excitement, we found our way to baggage claim, retrieved our heavy bags and hailed a taxi for the Mission guesthouse on West Ninety-second Street in the heart of New York City.

Looking down from our bedroom in the brownstone walk-up that was the guesthouse, we got a glimpse of our neighbors strolling around the crowded city in the early evening hours. We were already part of a new world, one much different than what we had ever known. The intensity of the day had us so wired up we could hardly sleep. Tucking David into bed, we lay awake talking into the early hours of the morning, reliving the experiences that had brought us to this time and place. An unknown future awaited us and it was very hard to fall asleep.

The next morning, we met Grace and Sam Pittman and their baby daughter Janet who would travel with us on the journey to Pakistan. Grace's parents had come from California to see them off, along with our Mission personnel director who had traveled from Chicago.

Our sea freight had been sent to New York ahead of time, and we spent part of the day making sure that it was being loaded on the ship. We also had to make last minute purchases. We bought traveler's checks and took a final look through our passports, documents, and tickets. By evening, we had assured ourselves that everything was in order. We were exhausted from lack of sleep as well as excitement and we slept soundly on that last night in America.

Awakening early on a new day, we closed our bags and headed for the port. Just before boarding the ship, our Mission representative, Dr. Ray Buker, gave a farewell prayer. A veteran missionary, he had served for many years in Burma, where there was a thriving Baptist community. We then boarded the *Steel King*, a "liberty ship" built more than a decade earlier during World War II that now served as a freighter for the Isthmian Shipping Line.

A crew member welcomed us aboard and showed us to our quarters. I was extremely grateful when I saw that we had been given a suite–a sleeping room with heavy steel bunk beds and a sitting room with steel and leather chairs, a sofa, tables, and lamps. We also had our own complete bathroom with stainless steel fixtures. This space was to be our home on the high seas for the next five weeks.

Meals were served each day in the officers' dining room. On that first evening, we met the only other passengers, two single missionary women, both nurses, traveling to Pakistan. We got acquainted with each other over a delicious dinner. Afterwards, we returned to our suite and unpacked. We were exhausted from the last few days and went to bed early. The gentle swaying of the ship in the harbor waters, an occasional blaring foghorn and the cold rain outside lulled us to sleep. The bunk beds proved to be comfortable. David cooperated and settled quickly into a deep sleep.

Sometime later, our peaceful sleep was rudely interrupted. The ship began to toss around, and I heard the bang, bang, bang of baby food jars crashing to the floor. We all awakened at once, startled and wondering what had happened. We had not been given a departure time but it did not take long for us to realize that the ship was leaving. It was eleven o'clock at night. Jumping off our bunks, we ran to the portholes in our cabin and, through the rain, watched the skyline with its millions of lights fade into the dark horizon. The Statue of Liberty receded into the distance as we finally reached the open sea.

Every day on the Atlantic Ocean was an exciting adventure and most of the time we were up with the sun. Occasionally, we spotted whales as they surfaced. Seeing another vessel in the vastness of the ocean exhilarated us with the knowledge that there were other human beings at sea, other people crossing to distant parts of the world. We stood on the deck at night and studied the skies, the start of a lasting interest in the constellations. During the day, we watched for weather changes. On that first day, the sea was rough and the ship reeled, leaving everyone, except David, woozy and nauseated. We were told that the North Atlantic was often rough during this time of year. Further out, the sea became calmer. Most of these days were long and uneventful. Still, the weeks at sea provided a reflective time of transition to our new life in Pakistan.

The director of our Mission had given us a list of required reading for the voyage, one of which was *Missions at the Crossroads*. The ship maintained a small library, and we indulged ourselves in some of its books as well. Sparky, the radio man, was an avid Scrabble player and we often played with him. With a toddler in tow, I had laundry to do, and railings around the engine room worked wonders as make-shift clothes drier. On Sundays, all the passengers—two single missionary nurses, two missionary couples, and two young children—met together for prayer and worship.

All of us were on deck when we first spotted land. In the distance, we saw the mountains of Spain on the north and Morocco to the south. We could see clearly a small Spanish town. Later on, we saw the large city of Centa on the North African coast. Looming over the horizon was the mighty Rock of Gibraltar. Overhead, flying low, French planes were maneuvering. We then sailed into the calm, blue, peaceful waters of the Mediterranean Sea.

Grace Kelly had recently married Prince Ranier of Monaco and their romance was dominating news reports at the time. The couple was supposed to be honeymooning in the Mediterranean. Although trying to spot them in their large luxurious yacht was a waste of time, we enjoyed looking out for them just the same. The next day we could see the North African city of Algiers and the silhouettes of the Muslim mosques against the sky—our first glance at the domes and minarets that characterized the world of Islam.

A few days later, the ship docked at Beirut, Lebanon. We arrived at four in the afternoon, received temporary visas, and were rowed ashore in a small boat. Snow-peaked Mount Hermon loomed in the distance. A friend met us, driving us directly to the Dog River and its nearby stones inscribed by invading kings. One of them was an inscription reportedly made by Sennacharib, dating back to Old Testament times. Just before dark, we were given a quick tour of the ancient Phoenician and Roman ruins at Byblos. The Lebanese people were friendly and hospitable. Beirut was a beautiful city with narrow streets, small shops and duty-free shopping. This was the first time we saw beggars on the streets and it seemed as if most of them were children. This was also the first time we saw Muslims bowing in public prayer. Everything was strange and different, and we had a lot to think and talk about when we returned to the ship at the end of every day.

The voyage from Beirut to Alexandria in Egypt took about twenty hours. Docking in mid-afternoon, we made arrangements for a city tour the following day. All six of us missionaries, along with the infant Janet and toddler David, disembarked for a tour of the large city of over a million inhabitants. Modern areas surprised us and seeing a department store was unexpected. However, museums, catacombs, Greek temple ruins, gardens, and King Farouk's palace surpassed all that we could imagine. The palace was a place of splendor and wealth, standing in stark contrast to the beggars on the streets of old Alexandria. To this day, I especially remember the gold fixtures in King Farouk's bathroom.

The following day, the *Steel King* steamed into Port Said where we waited our turn to proceed through the Suez Canal. Not long afterwards, the canal was nationalized by President Nasser, a move that electrified the Arab world and led to a brief but bloody war pitting

Israel, France, and Britain against the Egyptians. But that encounter was still some weeks away. We watched as a convoy of ships sailed north, identifying the various countries from which they came. One flew the Soviet flag, an alien and even threatening symbol for us in what was then the height of the Cold War. It was mid-day before our ship, along with others in a convoy, bound south for the Red Sea, entered the Suez Canal.

The canal was a narrow strip of water through mostly barren land. Along the way, there was a side canal and we slowly sailed into that to allow another convoy of ships to pass. We slept for most of the journey, waking to find ourselves in the Gulf of Suez and then the Red Sea. Captain Williams from Mississippi pointed out a line of mountains to the east, noting that one of them was Mount Sinai.

The next port of call was at Jeddah in Saudi Arabia. We were excited about the prospect of going ashore again. However, our spirits dampened when we learned we would not be allowed to leave the ship at all. It was *Ramadan*, the month of fasting when all faithful Muslims neither eat nor drink during the daylight hours. Smoking and sex are also prohibited. Muslim passengers in neighboring ships were allowed to enter Saudi Arabia to visit the holy sites in Mecca, just fifty miles away. Late in the afternoon, we sometimes observed a Saudi husband and wife visiting the harbor on an outing. The man walked ahead of the woman, who was dressed from head to toe in a black robe revealing only her eyes.

We stayed aboard the *Steel King* in Jeddah for nine days, watching local Saudis celebrate the beginning and end of the fast at the start and conclusion of each long day.

Even from a distance, it was clear that Islam permeated every aspect of Saudi society. During each of the five daily calls to prayer, men everywhere stopped, laid out their prayer mats, prostrated themselves toward Mecca and recited prayers in Arabic. Dock workers throughout the port lined up for these prayer times. The days were long and hot, and very few stevedores worked when the sun was shining with all its heat and intensity. They slept during the day, reserving the night hours to unload freight from the ship.

Bags of flour were unloaded, leaving a dusty film that, when mixed with damp sea air, left the deck slippery. At one point, David fell down and cut himself badly just under the chin. Fortunately, one of the missionary nurses on board knew exactly what to do. She gave him a butterfly stitch. And she calmed me, the anxious mother. It was a perfect way to take care of the wound, leaving no noticeable scar.

We were very happy to leave Jeddah, especially since our next port would be our final destination–Karachi. Our excitement continued to mount as we passed through the Red Sea, replete with Biblical references, and entered the Arabian Sea, a part of the Indian Ocean. We had already been on the high seas for nearly five weeks. The hot and humid weather kept us inside for most of the time. We had Bible studies and prayer times together. We read every book and magazine we could lay our hands on, played Scrabble and Rook, and had long discussions about what might lie ahead in Pakistan. When, finally, our ship was nearing Karachi, we found it hard to believe we were actually arriving.

The *Steel King* entered Karachi harbor, guided by a pilot boat. Small boats dotted about here and there with occupants colorfully dressed, all seemingly happy and joyful. Along the pier, crowds of people walked about, all dressed in holiday finery. *Ramadan* was over and *Eid* celebrations were now underway.

Anxiously looking into the throngs of people, it was difficult for us to find an expected American face. Suddenly, a small car sped around the corner and parked. Two men who were clearly not Pakistani stepped out. What a relief! We were being met after all!

We invited our two missionary colleagues to have dinner with us on the ship. A good, home-style American meal was just what they needed. They also devoured our five-week-old *Time* magazine from cover to cover. At that time, both American cuisine and news from the United States were in scant supply in Pakistan.

Unloading the *Steel King*, including our baggage from the ship's hold, took longer than we had thought. We dreaded facing customs officials, having been warned ahead of time of what we might expect.

All our earthly possessions had been carefully packed in steel barrels and wood crates, including clothes, household items, books, toys for a growing boy, and even luxury items such as coffee and cocoa. One friend had made bookcases for us from Georgia pine. They were two identical cases, packed with toilet paper and other light items, and bound together by steel bands. We also planned to use the refrigerator and stove crates as cupboards. Custom duties would be levied on each item that the customs official deemed worthy of tax. We had made a heroic effort to stay within the taxable limits, just as we had fit everything into the allowable cubic feet allocated by the Isthmian Shipping Line for our journey to Pakistan.

Much to our relief, our colleagues had arranged for a shipping agent to clear our possessions through customs. His name was Mr. Butt and he came on board with four or five officials from the customs department, each dressed in stiffly starched, white shirts, Bermuda shorts, stockings and polished shoes. The customs officials smiled perfunctorily, and then we got down to business in the dining room of the ship. There were long forms to fill out and sign. Hu answered each question and signed the papers. It was over–and, to our huge surprise and relief, our baggage was declared duty free, and we were not charged even a single *paisa*.

Since the ship was not sailing for a couple more days, Captain Williams invited us to remain on board. We gladly accepted his offer. After everything was cleared and we were free to leave, we suddenly felt reluctant to step on shore. The *Steel King* had been our home for five weeks and it was hard to say good-bye.

Herbie, the ship's cook, came to us with a load of goodies. He told us that we didn't really know what we were getting ourselves into and wanted to give us a parting gift of peanut butter, crackers, candy, and other useful items. The ship's crew all bade us farewell and we departed for the home of missionary colleagues who had extra space for people like us. Little David and I, along with Grace and baby Janet, stayed with a young Baptist couple from Oklahoma, and Hu and Sam stayed with a Church Missionary Society couple from New Zealand. We were entering the hottest part of the year, and the men slept outside under mosquito nets to take advantage of the cool evening breeze. Later, Hu told me that one of his lasting memories of our arrival was the crows in the trees, cawing in a lush green garden amidst the noise of the busy city outside.

The big city of Karachi offered much more in consumer goods than we had expected. Opening bank accounts, exchanging money, making reservations for the train trip up country, and shopping took up a lot of time. I was amazed at the lovely home and adequate living conditions that our friends enjoyed. I was also pleasantly surprised to see the table set with fine china and beautiful linens. Our baggage contained a set of thick melamine dinnerware that would grace our table for a number of years, a reminder that living in the interior of the country would be quite different. Years later, however, we bought a beautiful set of china, made in what was then Czechoslovakia, complete with a tea and coffee set. Our arrival in Pakistan was an important milestone in the direction our lives were taking. The days ahead would unfold with many more new experiences, each different than the last. Our voyage across several oceans had just ended; our journey into the interior of Pakistan was about to begin.

Chapter Two

WHEELS

One remarkable feature about Pakistan in the mid 1950s was the multitude of ways that people and possessions traveled from place to place. Disembarking at the port of Karachi after five weeks at sea, we were immediately confronted by some of the more common forms of transport–rickshaws, camel carts, donkey carts and horse drawn carriages.

Our first ride through Karachi was on a beautiful horse-drawn Victorian Carriage built during British times. It had four wheels and two leather upholstered seats facing each other. The driver, in his own seat and resplendent in a clean uniform and turban, was courteous and helpful as we loaded our cabin luggage and then climbed aboard for the journey into the city.

The streets of Karachi were jammed with taxis, trucks, and buses, all honking horns and belching clouds of exhaust. Motor cycles wove in and out of the congested traffic, competing for space with small horse-drawn *tongas* and taxis.

The trucks and buses especially stood out because of the colorful paintings which adorned them–landscapes, flowers, animals, popular proverbs, and verses from their poets or whatever else struck the fancy of the artist. Over the years that we lived in Pakistan, the scenes became even more elaborate, depicting movie stars, battles, mythical creatures and other fantastic images. Even today, the tradition of painting trucks in Pakistan has continued, reflecting a vibrant folk art that reveals the country in especially creative and intriguing ways.

Karachi, at that time, also had bicycle rickshaws, a three-wheeled contraption in which the operator peddled furiously at the front, pulling two uncomfortably seated passengers in the carriage behind. This form of transport, still common in some parts of East Asia and South Asia, was eventually replaced by the motor rickshaws which also transported up to two passengers but made much more noise.

Later, when we reached the hill station of Murree in the north, we encountered another form of human-drawn rickshaw, operated by four Kashmiri *coolies*- two at the front pulling and two at the back pushing. Harking back to the days of the British Raj, this type of transport seemed especially demeaning and was eventually banned.

—

Many books have been written about the trains of the Indian sub-continent. When we arrived in Pakistan in the mid 1950s, most trains were still being powered by coal-fired steam engines. A few years later, diesel engines were introduced. We rode countless miles on Pakistan's trains and to this day the haunting sounds of a train whistle, the chug-chug of the steam engine and the clackity-clack of the railway carriage wheels echo in my memory.

Long-distance journeys during our early years in Pakistan almost always involved trains. The British left a well-functioning train system in Pakistan. Even as late as the 1950s, much of the rail service was still being run by Anglo-Indians and the coaches still carried the name "Northwestern Railways," denoting that part of northwest India which became Pakistan. Later, of course, the name became "Pakistan Railways."

Travel classes were well established, no doubt based partly on the caste system which dominated life in South Asia for centuries and partly on the class system which the British brought with them during the eighteenth century.

First Class was, of course, the most luxurious, featuring a small private compartment with leather upholstery. For overnight travel, the seating converted into beds, with clean sheets provided for a small additional price. Other amenities included food service, cleaners, and an English style toilet with a stainless steel wash basin. In later years, air conditioning was introduced as well.

Then there was Second Class. Less expensive than First Class, but less crowded and more comfortable than Third Class, this became our preferred mode of transport. The compartments were large and often filled to capacity. During the day, this meant about twelve passengers, though sometimes more crowded in. At night, capacity was reduced to the six sleeping passengers who had reservations. Each had a bunk of his or her own for sleeping.

Our first long overland journey in Pakistan, from Karachi to Rawalpindi, was in a Second Class railway carriage. It took thirty-six hours. No doubt the arrival of five American adults along with two children and their accompanied baggage was an unusual sight. We carried toilet paper as well as our own boiled drinking water in large clay jugs. A colleague had also arranged for a large block of ice to be placed in a tin tub in the middle of the compartment. With the overhead fan blowing down upon it, we benefited from a sort of primitive, improvised air conditioning system, a welcomed addition given that we were also traveling during the hottest part of the year.

The repeated clackety-clack of the moving train should have been enough to lull me to sleep. However, dust filtered through the tightly closed windows. At every stop along the way, hawkers walked up and down the platform, shouting in loud voices as they sold hot tea and various kinds of food which as yet we had not identified. Although extremely careful to drink only boiled water and eat only the food we brought with us, I began to feel sick. Frequent visits to the toilet and nausea kept me awake. By morning I had developed a fever. The exciting newness of all I was experiencing began to wear off. Reality had begun to set in, including the fact that disease was all around us. Sickness and ill health, too, would be a regular part of our life in Pakistan.

After a day and a half, we finally arrived at our destination, the *cantonment* town of Rawalpindi in the north of the country. Located at the edge of the Himalayas, it was also a stopping off point on the road to Kashmir. We were met by a colleague and crowded into his jeep for the forty-mile journey into the Murree Hills. At seven thousand feet, Murree had been established by the British exactly a century earlier as a hill station, a place for rest and recuperation from the rigors of the hot plains below. We too were revived by the friendly welcome, cold drinking water, and cool mountain air. David, like a bird out of a cage, ran around with a freedom that he had not enjoyed for a long time–and promptly tumbled down a flight of concrete steps, emerging with a bump the size of a goose egg on his head.

―

The ensuing years and experience taught us to travel with less fuss and more frequency. When money was tight, we lowered our class of train travel, on occasion traveling Inter Class or Third Class, the main difference being that Inter Class was slightly more expensive and slightly less crowded than Third.

Both Inter Class and Third Class contained long slatted wooden seats where passengers crowded together–along with smelly body odors, stench from the eastern-style floor toilet, smoke from local cigarettes and *hookahs*, crying babies and dust blowing endlessly through open windows. Everyone carried their own *bister* for sleeping.

Once we were invited to attend a wedding involving a village headman living in northern Punjab. Concerned over our budget, we chose to downgrade and traveled Third Class. We staked out our space on two upper bunks and spent most of the trip there, reading or trying to doze. Occasionally, at one of the frequent stops, Hu would stretch his legs and buy some refreshments on the bustling station platform.

Throughout the journey, a fan above droned out an endless but a welcomed hum. One of the fans had been removed and only a steel bolt was protruding from the ceiling. After a short stop, the train pulled out of the station. Hu returned to the upper bunk. He had to use the lower bunk as a step. With one foot firmly planted on the lower bunk he jumped upward. His head hit against the protruding bolt.

Immediately, he winced in pain and I saw blood streaming down his face. I almost panicked. I knew head injuries cause prolific bleeding, but I was scared. This was serious. I even thought of pulling the emergency lever to stop the train. Attempting to stop the flow of blood, I applied our bed sheet and mopped up the blood as best I could. Fellow travelers looked on at my futile efforts. Nothing seemed to work.

"Madam, we have a remedy for such situations," one soft-spoken fellow traveler suddenly said. "If you will allow me, I think I can stop the bleeding."

What to do? What I was doing obviously was not working. Apprehensively, I gave him permission to take over and apply a folk remedy of his own.

He tore a piece of silk from his wife's scarf, threw it on the floor, struck a match and burned it to ashes. He then took the ashes and placed them along the cut in Hu's head. Almost immediately, the bleeding stopped!

I was grateful for his help in our time of emergency. Hu felt pain and the injury continued to ooze slightly but the emergency was over.

Later, we had an opportunity to consult with a missionary doctor. He cleaned the injury and stitched the wound. Thankfully Hu's hair was thick, and we managed to comb his hair over the injury and proceed to the wedding. As far as we know, no one ever noticed. When we finally returned home, he took antibiotics to deal with a beginning infection. A lasting scar reminds us always of that trip.

—

Most of the time, when we traveled together, we chose a general compartment. This decision meant that men sat in the compartment with us by day and slept with us at night. The men enjoyed the children and Hu enjoyed talking with the men.

Local women never traveled in the general compartments. Special carriages called *zenana* were reserved for women on every train. Men were not allowed to travel in these carriages, though small male children were permitted to accompany their mothers and other female relatives. Whenever the train stopped, the male relatives traveling in other carriages would come by to check on their women.

I always chose to book a seat in the *zenana* when traveling alone. Once my daughter Nancy and I were on a short trip, and we climbed into the always crowded women's section. As usual, children outnumbered the women. We managed to find a place to sit together and waited for the train to pull out of the station. Just as the train pulled away from the platform, a man hopped onto the step and tried to get into the door. I got up and locked the door from inside. After all, it was an established custom; men were not allowed to travel in these compartments reserved exclusively for women and children. Perhaps he was a relative of one of the women travelers. I didn't know. But I knew he would not come in. I had read accounts of men who had entered these sacred compartments only to terrorize and even abuse women.

A couple of women wanted to unlock the door. The train gained speed very quickly, and I began to feel responsible should he fall off the train and get killed. However, I did not give in. I was grateful and relieved when the train, after some time, pulled into another station and stopped. The man hopped off and was lost in the crowd, obviously not related to any of the women aboard.

Another time, a colleague and close friend of mine and I took a journey by train to Quetta, a hill station and *cantonment* town in the western part of the country near the border with Afghanistan. Of course, as women traveling without a male escort we chose the ladies' compartment. It was not at all crowded in Second Class. The other women were quietly reserved. They looked–rather they stared--at us often, trying to figure us out. As usual, we both were wearing Pakistani clothes–*shalwar, khameez, duputta*. I often wore rather large sun glasses. This habit was my adaptation to the culture where women always veiled themselves in a *burka* when venturing outside their home.

On this trip, our outfits were rather pretty and stylish. By local standards, we looked perhaps a little exotic, taking on the appearance of sophisticated city people. After some time, we decided to speak to the women in their language. We asked about them, why they were going to Quetta, how many children they had and what their family situation was like. After awhile, they began to ask us questions. We then did something quite out of character for both of us. We were having a good time and quite honestly felt euphoric about the opportunity to travel this long distance on our own.

We were silly. When asked our names, we gave our names as two of Pakistan's most famous movie actresses. We kept up this little charade for quite some time. We felt a bit guilty when we realized our charade might actually be believable. They laughed with us when we told them it was all in fun. We never had such fun or opportunities to interact with Pakistani women when we traveled with our husbands in the general compartment.

———

At the beginning of every summer we embarked more than 700 miles on a train trip north to the mountains. Like the generations of British on the Indian subcontinent before us, we rented cottages in the cool hills with our children. Hu escorted and settled me into the house and returned to the hot and dusty plains to continue working.

A move like this always involved extra baggage. We needed to set up a separate household during these weeks away. Therefore, we traveled with boxes of pots and pans, household linens, and whatever else we needed for our comfort.

This time away from the extreme heat provided us an opportunity to spend time with our children, who attended the boarding school established for missionary children in Murree. On arrival we settled into our cottage and collected our children from boarding. They continued in school while living at home and rode the school bus daily.

Except for the absence of Hu, these were normal months for us. The community of missionaries from Europe, North America, Australia and New Zealand created many aspects of home, including PTA, regular church services and Sunday school in English. We enjoyed participating in events that involved our children such as dramas, recitals and sports events. Hu spent a short time with us at the beginning and end of each summer.

The logistics for our annual train journey north were sometimes complicated. Often we traveled with colleagues. One such trip included not only our family but two single women, two cooks and their families, and two dogs. Knowing that in one station, Rohri Junction, we would have to wait for hours for a connecting train we were prepared! Among our baggage we had included an old fashioned ice cream churn and the necessary ingredients to make a gallon of ice cream.

As soon as we arrived in Rohri, we found a place in the large waiting room. Then we put the ingredients together, found a block of ice to chip up, and took turns at the handle of the ice cream churn. I can only imagine what the fellow travelers around us must have thought. Most probably, we looked like aliens from outer space with our pets, small children and mounds of baggage—and all the equipment needed to make homemade ice cream. I remember dumping a can of expensive imported pineapple into the mixture. The weather was hot, very hot.

None of us had ever enjoyed homemade ice cream as much as we did that hot day in the Rohri Railway station.

———

Another time we boarded a train after dark at Hyderabad. This time it was Hu, myself, and our dog, a poodle we called Dixie. The compartment was small. Just outside was a narrow corridor that connected to another compartment. It was night and our fellow travelers had already stretched out on their bunks to go to sleep. We immediately prepared our own beds on the remaining lower bunks.

My bunk was alongside the corridor. I lowered the windows. They could not be locked. Our luggage was neatly stacked under the bunks. My purse, a rather large leather bag I had bought on a trip to Kabul, Afghanistan some time before, stayed with me. I nestled it under my arm like a pillow and went off to sleep.

A short time later, I felt my bag being tugged away from me. I opened my eyes to see it disappearing out the window.

"*Chor, chor,*" I screamed, "Thief, thief."

Immediately, Dixie began to bark and the men on the upper bunks sat up. Hu jumped up from his bunk and tried to calm me.

"Everything I own is in that bag!" I yelled dramatically.

Normally, I tucked the few pieces of jewelry I owned in my bag, believing it would be safer than in other suitcases. I remained awake, moaning about my loss. Not only was I wide awake, but I was angry, and devastated. How could I be violated in such a way while riding on a train?

Shortly, the train pulled into another station and stopped. I glared outside onto the lighted platform as crowds milled about, some passengers disembarking while others climbed into the train carriages. Suddenly, I saw a man with my bag! Yes indeed, my bag. I jumped up, stuck my head out the window and screamed to the top of my voice in Urdu.

"That man has my bag! That man is a thief! Catch that man. He has my bag."

In a moment, he handed the bag back to me and slipped off into the darkness. I could not believe my eyes. Immediately I searched my bag to see what was missing. In truth, on this occasion I had packed the bag only with toilet articles needed for the journey, neither jewelry nor other valuable items. The thief, if he had looked, must have been terribly disappointed with the contents of this "rich American's" purse. Perhaps this is the reason he returned it so quickly.

I was more than glad when the sun came up the next morning. Word had spread throughout the train that a gang of robbers had boarded in Hyderabad and proceeded to methodically ransack passengers, carriage by carriage, as they slept. Unfortunately, some passengers suffered great loss at the hands of the thieves.

———

Buses were another important part of the Pakistani landscape. They plied the small back roads as well as the national highways. Because of the size and speed of their vehicles, the bus drivers had special mystique. It was as if they literally owned the roads.

We always said one risks life and limb when traveling on the roads of Pakistan. Some years ago, an American newspaper even alluded to this in a headline: "Never Is a Man Nearer his Maker than on the Grand Trunk Road." Local newspapers often featured stories about head on collisions or buses that had toppled off mountainsides or into rivers and canals, sometimes killing dozens at a time.

As a general rule, we did not travel by bus. However, Hu and the boys would sometimes take short bus journeys to neighboring towns. As in trains, there was always a special section reserved for women. Often, their space was enclosed by iron bars that formed a small cage in the front of the bus, just behind the driver. The women, completely covered in a *burka,* would jam themselves into the small cubicle, children and baggage in tow.

I never understood how local women managed to stay alive when traveling this way, especially in hot weather. I had one short experience sitting in the women's section of one of these buses, joining several locals in my allotted seat within the small barred cubicle that for all practical purposes was a cage. I immediately vowed I would never, ever travel this way again.

—

Although we did not ride trucks, they represented another important part of the transport system in Pakistan. If bus drivers viewed themselves as "kings of the road," truck drivers thought of themselves as "emperors of the highways." They traveled very fast up and down the roads throughout Pakistan, sometimes fortified with opium or other narcotics for an especially long journey. We suspected the bus drivers did the same.

Now, painted buses are gradually disappearing from Pakistan, having been replaced by modern coaches from Korea. However, the colorfully decorated trucks remain. The truck drivers sometimes include paintings of their children along with the movie stars, mythical figures, and beautiful scenes that add both color and creativity to the roads of Pakistan.

In fact, perhaps nothing captures the ethos of urban working class Pakistan more than the painted trucks. The themes and styles change over time, but the painted slogans and proverbs are always insightful. *"Load Sukkur, unload Larkana, that is my life's journey,"* reads one of them. *"Sorry, I am in a race against time,"* reads another. Others are equally interesting, entertaining, and revealing: *"Pray for me, my beloved;" "Think of me when spring comes to the garden;" "A curse on the selfish;" "What a life, what a world, wherever you look, injustice rules;"* and *"Who says I will die when death comes – I am a driver and I will twist and turn and get away."*

Where there are trucks, there are also truck stops. Tea shops, blaring music, and rope strung beds provide welcome relief for weary drivers as well as an opportunity for the trucks to cool off. In our travels by road, often we would stop at a truck stop to buy hot tea or freshly-baked flat bread referred to as *nan* or *chappati*. The children especially enjoyed spreading peanut butter and jelly on the local bread, making for a delicious sandwich. Peanut butter and a banana rolled in bread were equally delicious. Although we had never heard of a "wrap" of any kind, we had created our own, long before the idea hit the fast food stalls of America.

—

During the summer months in Murree and when our children were small, we hired little donkeys for them to ride. Walking down the hill from our house was fun. For them to walk back up the hill following shopping or church was just too much. The donkey owners were clever. They had made little saddle seats to fit over the donkey. Children fit in very well and rode safely. Otherwise, their tired little legs may have given out and we would have had to carry them.

When the children became too big for the donkeys, there were horses waiting to transport them up the hill. I even chose to ride a horse a few times when walking seemed too difficult. Weekends were times to explore the nearby countryside and horses became our way of getting around. On a number of occasions, we were invited into some of the village homes that dotted the mountainside. Getting there on winding mountain paths was tricky. Horses seemed to have better footing than humans, especially on difficult mountain slopes.

—

An important and common conveyance for the village folk in those years was the bullock cart. Essentially, it consisted of a wooden platform with two wooden wheels that, as they turned on a wooden axle, made a loud, squeaking noise. Two oxen were hitched to the cart. These animals were used to haul grain from the village to market towns. Ox carts, like camel carts, often traveled in caravans. Once or twice, when traveling down the highway, we stopped while our children, with permission from the driver, boarded the carts to experience yet another form of transportation. Although grain was hauled on these carts, families also rode on them.

This ancient cart came to our rescue once. We were deep into a rural area where there were really no roads; just trails for ox carts. Our Land Rover got stuck in a bog. The more we tried to get out, the deeper the wheels sank. Villagers came to our rescue. They filled the ruts with sticks and stones. They pushed. The tires only spun around and around. One of the village men came up with a brilliant idea; he ran across the field where a farmer was plowing with his oxen. In just a few minutes he returned with the oxen. Hitching the oxen to our Land

Rover worked like a charm. Very quickly, the oxen pulled our vehicle out of the bog and we were on our way. The villagers applauded as we left.

Camel caravans, pulling carts of freight, traveled mostly at night. A dozen or more carts at a time moved quietly along the main highway. Rubber tires were used for wheels so the only noise was the tinkling of the small bells that were sometimes attached to the necks or ankles of the camels. Often asleep, the driver lay stretched out on top of his baggage. A kerosene lantern hung between the wheels at the back of every cart. We celebrated David's birthday one year with a camel cart hayride. It was easy to hire the cart and the driver loaded it with hay. We chose to go outside of town to a nearby canal bank. It was cold and dark and we built a fire, roasting homemade marshmallows.

Years later, the long lines of ox carts and camel carts that used to be such an essential part of the Sindhi landscape have largely disappeared. While animal-drawn transport, whether pulled by camels, donkeys, horses, or oxen, still operates in parts of rural Pakistan, the long-haul trips of the past are by now quite rare. It has become cheaper to rely on trucks, buses, and vans to haul people and produce, especially over long distances. Just as mass-produced plastic containers have largely replaced pottery in Pakistan, animal traction, too, is becoming a thing of the past.

—

We did not have our own vehicle during our first four years in Pakistan. However, colleagues were kind enough to lend us their Land Rover from time to time. One such trip involved a journey to Kabul in neighboring Afghanistan, a remote and isolated country that had only recently opened itself up to foreign visitors.

We left Murree early in the morning and traveled along the crowded Grand Trunk Road to Peshawar where we obtained the necessary documents for our onward journey into Afghanistan. The two boys were perched on top of the luggage in the back of the Land Rover. David was especially interested in everything he saw along the way and refused to lie down in the back. Most of the time, he sat on my lap so that he could have a window view.

The trip from Peshawar to Kabul took us through the Khyber Pass, across the plains of Jalalabad and then through a narrow gorge where in the nineteenth century an entire British army unit had been butchered by the Afghans. The scenery was always changing and sometimes breathtaking, with fort-like houses clinging to distant ridges.

It seemed as though every man—there were almost no women to be seen—had a gun. The frontier people looked strange and somewhat alarming with weapons and bandoliers hanging over their shoulders along with their full-flowing clothes, beards, and head coverings. They had defeated the British and, in later decades, would defeat the Soviets. At the time, I could not imagine that these Pushtun tribesmen would eventually form the base of the Taliban, taking on the might of the U.S. army as well.

The road was narrow, rocky, and unpaved much of the way. In some places, it seemed to be just a trail. David was very excited when he saw forts dotting the tops of the barren mountains. For my part, I did not relax at what seemed like a totally alien territory.

The road became even worse as we journeyed onward through Afghanistan. Hu had to put the Land Rover into four wheel drive as we crossed streams and climbed mountains. We noticed heavy Soviet equipment in places, busily building a new road from the border post at Torkham to Kabul. At one point, the road was very narrow and a big imposing Soviet vehicle came so close that we actually scraped each other, without damage although a little paint rubbed off onto our vehicle.

After spending hours on the road, we stopped along the way to picnic and to stretch our legs. I was afraid to get out of the car. I don't know why I was afraid. Everything was strange. I knew that, without a doubt, unseen eyes were always on us, following our every move. I also concluded on this trip that I would never find a rock or bush big enough for me to hide behind, ensuring I would have to undertake the entire journey without a toilet stop. Why hadn't I thought of taking a full white *burka* for just this need? It would have made an instant tent.

We had been traveling a long time and the sun was high in the sky. Suddenly, the car stopped in the middle of nowhere. Hu is not and was never a mechanic. We both looked at each other. He lifted the hood, tinkered with some wires and tried to start the engine. It refused to start. Again, we looked at each other in bewilderment and possibly alarm.

Very little traffic was on the road. Now and then a truck laden with goods being hauled from Peshawar to Kabul would come along. I prayed that one of these would stop. And one did. The truck drivers are great mechanics. They know how to fix just about anything. We don't know what he did, but he fiddled with the wires and managed to start the engine, allowing us to continue on our way. I realized then that the Afghans, too, are very friendly and helpful.

The sun was setting as we reached the high plain of Kabul, surrounded by mountains. It was springtime, the nearby mountains were covered in snow and the views in every direction were breathtaking. By the time we reached the city, the sun had sunk behind the distant peaks and it was dark. With a little difficulty we made our way through the narrow streets to the home of our American hosts. I could hardly extract myself from the Land Rover. It seemed almost impossible to straighten my back. Hobbling into the house, I was relieved to find a clean, western style toilet. I was glad to be in Kabul.

———

In later years, we bought a Land Rover of our own, making the long journey from Upper Sindh to Murree each year by road rather than by train. It was fun and certainly educational to go by road. We saw Pakistan as we never would have seen it. Also, we met and often stayed with other missionary friends along the way, learning more about their work.

Invariably, we traveled with our pets – a dog and a cat. One cat ran away when we stopped to picnic along the way. Unable to find the cat we had to leave without it. The dog traveled well. We had a cage for the animals and both the cat and dog traveled together. Whenever we stopped, onlookers gawked with astonishment to see the two, peacefully coexisting in the same cage. Not that we needed protection, but I felt safer when we had the dog with us.

Recalling those long trips north, there are two incidents that especially stand out. The first involved an overnight with missionary friends in Punjab. Their courtyard was surrounded by a low wall and a see-through gate. I was used to a very high brick wall, probably 10-12 feet high, and a very thick wooden door opening into our courtyard from the street. I always felt safe. However, on that night I felt vulnerable.

Each of us—Hu, David and I—had our own *charpai*, strung with rope and a thin cotton mattress. Mosquito nets tied to bamboo poles were attached to each bed. David's cot was in the middle, with Hu's bed on one side and mine on the other. For some reason, I always had this nagging maternal fear David might be kidnapped. He was a handsome child, with very dark hair, dark eyes and a deep olive complexion. In fact, he could easily have been mistaken for a Pakistani child. I always kept my eyes on him and insisted he never go outside our courtyard without an adult.

We loved sleeping outside in the hot weather. Everyone did. In our own home, we slept on our flat roof top, high above the noise of the street. However, in this home there was no roof for sleeping. The beds were on the ground, just off the street behind low walls. I was restless. During the night, I suddenly woke up and looked over to check on David. He was not there. He was gone! He was not in his bed. It was all I could do to keep from screaming. I got out of bed quietly and awakened Hu.

"David is gone," I said. "David is not in his bed!"

Alarmed, we both got up and began to look around. There must have been a little moon light or perhaps a dim street light. Worried, we were ready to awaken our hosts and alert them. However, looking down at David's bed again I noticed his mosquito net hanging down on one side. A closer look revealed David sleeping soundly as though he was in a hammock. Quickly retrieving him, I hugged him close and snuggled with him in my bed for the remainder of the night.

—

Another episode on the road from Murree to Sindh also scared me. When we traveled we always took a picnic lunch. Nothing was available along the way. Besides, we needed to stop on the roadside, give the children a break as well as exercise our own legs. We looked for a shady place which was often alongside a canal bank, an oasis indeed. Finally we found such a place. Immediately Hu took the children and the pets and went off to a nearby field to allow them to run about.

I pulled out the picnic basket, laid out a cloth and began to prepare the lunch. I looked in vain for the can opener. Distressed, I went to the car and found a small emergency kit that included a pocket knife. I plunged the knife into the can and missed. Blood spurted from my wrist and I knew at once I had severed an artery. Grabbing my wrist, I applied pressure and shouted for Hu to come. He came immediately, the children and pets trailing behind. The blood covering my dress frightened the children. Hu wanted to apply a tourniquet. I vetoed the idea, suggesting instead that we load the car and find the nearest hospital.

I kept applying pressure, probably far too much. Periodically, I felt sick and kept my head down to my knees. Somewhere along the way we lost the muffler off the exhaust pipe, and the Land Rover sounded very much like an airplane roaring down the road. We were miles from a hospital. It was mid afternoon and very hot. Help seemed a long, long way away.

Finally, we reached the town of Rahimyarkhan in southern Punjab. We looked for and found the civil hospital and drove into the courtyard. The attendant met us, saw our circumstance and went for the doctor. The doctor came and took over. A nurse in a starched white uniform appeared and began to sterilize instruments. I was led into an operating room and told to lie down on the table. Still feeling nauseous, I did what I was told to do.

Minutes later, the doctor was ready to take a stitch to seal the severed artery. First he wanted to inject a local anesthesia. I assured him I was able to take the stitch without anesthesia. I did not want two needle pricks when I could get by with one!

With professionalism and gentleness an anonymous civil surgeon in a small provincial hospital in southern Punjab literally saved my life. We apologized several times for interrupting his afternoon rest. He provided tea and graciously offered any service we might require. He refused payment. We exchanged pleasantries and continued on our way.

—

While living in small towns in Upper Sindh, Hu got around on a bicycle or used our Land Rover. The boys usually traveled around town on their bicycles as well. Local men and boys also relied on bicycles. On occasion, we even saw a father with three or four children and his *burka*-clad wife moving around town on a single bicycle.

Unfortunately, neither Nancy nor I could use a bicycle. As females and in keeping with local custom, we went by *tonga*, a simple two wheeled horse-drawn carriage that is seen even today on the streets of provincial towns in Pakistan. These reminded me somewhat of pictures I had seen of buggies that my grandparents rode in. However, in Pakistan there was a front seat for the driver while passengers sat in the back, facing backwards. These carriages also had a canvas canopy to protect passengers from the blazing sun.

I relied on a *tonga* to get me around town when visiting my Muslim friends. It was quick, cheap, and simple. Also, it was less visible than the Land Rover. Custom dictated that women never go outside alone. Our male servant accompanied me. He always sat in the front seat with the driver. Once I was safely inside the courtyard of my friends' homes, he either returned home or hung around with other servants until I was ready to go home. When I was ready, he was always waiting for me. He took care of calling for the *tonga* as well as paying him.

A child was also an acceptable escort and one or more of my children enjoyed these excursions. The women I visited loved having them come with me. I distinctly remember one occasion when I took Jonathan with me to a friend's house. The women were discussing an upcoming event and wanted me to attend. Most of the conversation was in Sindhi, which I could easily follow. In fact, the women were discussing Jonathan. The question raised was, "Is he now too mature to invite to an event like this?"

A certain gray area separates childhood from adolescence in traditional Pakistani homes. Children move easily between the world of women and the world of men but adolescents cannot. Socially, once a child reaches puberty, girls live out the rest of their lives in a woman's world while young men enter the world of men.

Jonathan was growing up but had not yet reached adolescence, hence the dilemma as to whether he should be included.

One woman answered, "He does not yet have fuzz on his face, so it is all right for him to come."

Thus, my invitation included Jonathan and Nancy. Of course David, having grown fuzz, was no longer even considered. Should men be invited, David would have gone with his dad.

———

During the latter part of our years in Pakistan we lived in two large cities, Hyderabad and Karachi. We gave up the Land Rover and bought sedans, more suitable to city driving. In Hyderabad, we drove a used Peugeot. It provided useful service for several years. In Karachi, we opted for a small Nissan Sunny which was suitable for weaving in and out of the thick traffic.

Although I maintained a Pakistani driver's license, I left the driving up to Hu. I preferred to call a motor rickshaw to drive me around town. These three-wheeled vehicles were incredibly noisy, emitting a loud rat-tat-tat sound, and occasionally backfiring in what sounded like gun fire or a small explosion. The fumes were awful. I pulled my thin *duputta* over my face to keep from breathing the fumes directly. Two people could squeeze tightly into the back seat while the driver, seated in front, seemed to make up his own rules as he took on all the traffic. One Pakistani friend told me the one rule of the road is to avoid eye contact with another driver. The other driver will think you don't see him and will get out of your way.

Crossing a busy Karachi road by foot was perhaps the most dangerous moment of all. Traffic weaved in every direction and at every speed, ranging from camel carts to donkey carts to rickshaws to sport cars and motor bikes. Once I gamely tried to cross a very wide street I thought was clear. To my horror, a motorcycle was suddenly speeding in my direction. I nearly froze in the middle of the street. To avoid hitting me, the cyclist veered, lost control and tumbled to the ground. I saw a mirror from the cycle fly through the air. I ran as fast as I could to the other side and hit a wall, bruising myself all over. The cyclist cursed me, picked up his broken mirror and sped off. I learned later that a woman had been hit by a speeding vehicle on the same street just a week before and ended up in the hospital with multiple injuries.

I came to dread every street crossing. Once I had to cross the street to visit a shop on the other side. I walked to the corner and waited for the lights. I stood there and the lights changed a number of times, yet I could not bring myself to cross. Cars, rickshaws, buses, and motorcycles moved in every direction. I was scared. Ultimately I hailed a motor rickshaw and asked the driver to take me all of twenty yards, safely across the street. I paid him, leaving him with his own thoughts about this foreign woman and her fears about the traffic in Karachi.

———

We were thrilled when air travel made its entrance in the 1960's into the interior of the country. The nearest airport for us at that time was located outside Sukkur, about 24 miles away. The planes used for domestic flights by Pakistan International Airlines were Dutch-built Fokkers. The arrival of the Fokker turbo props meant that, in an emergency, we could reach our children, who were away in boarding school, on the same day, rather than having to take a very long trip by train or car.

One such emergency occurred when Jonathan was away in boarding. He had a medical problem that possibly required surgery. We made arrangements for him to travel to Lahore for consultation with an American specialist working in a large mission hospital. Hu took the train up to meet him. I remained at home.

We had decided that, should surgery be required, I would take a plane to arrive in time for the operation. Only a few people had telephones at the time, and cell phones had not yet been invented. On occasions such as this, we had to rely on telegrams.

"Jonathan needs surgery. Pick up your ticket at PIA in Sukkur," stated the cryptic telegram that Hu sent from Lahore.

Suddenly, I was thrown into a dilemma we had not foreseen. How would I reach Sukkur, twenty five miles away? All of our missionary colleagues were out of town. What should I do? To hire a taxi and take off on my own was unthinkable. A strict custom for Muslim women is that they do not go outside their home alone. There must be an escort. Anyway, a taxi was not acceptable for me, a foreign woman in a rural area.

I thought of a good friend, a Muslim woman whom I knew quite well. She was from a leading family in town. We had a close friendship. I sat down and wrote her a short note, explaining my unusual circumstances and asked for her help. Our servant hopped on his bicycle and went across town delivering my note to her home. Very shortly, he returned. My worries were over. She told me that her driver would be at my door within the hour. He had instructions to assist me in any way I needed him. He also received instructions to stay with me all the time until I was on the plane. There was no need for my servant to accompany me. I was perfectly safe with the family's driver.

I arrived in Lahore that afternoon, met by Hu at the airport and we both were present for Jonathan's thoracic surgery. The American specialist performed the surgery and his loving wife and young daughters took special care of us. We had entered another mode of modern transportation in Pakistan. Distances that once seemed so large suddenly became smaller.

———

The introduction of air travel also provided opportunity for our children to come home for short visits during the boarding term. Previously, during short breaks in the school year, they were unable to come because of the distance and time. On one occasion when they had a long week-end break, we drove to Quetta, Baluchistan's provincial capital and had them fly to meet us there. We spent several days in the nearby town of Ziarat, situated in a scenic valley covered in juniper forests.

Sir Henry Holland, a British eye surgeon who spent his life giving sight to the blind across Baluchistan, had built a vacation cottage in Ziarat. It was an austere structure with two bedrooms, bath, sitting room, dining room, kitchen and a long open verandah. He used it as a vacation retreat during his many years in the country. His two sons, Henry and Harry, followed in his footsteps as missionary doctors to Pakistan and used the cottage for vacations as well.

The scene awaiting us hearkened back to the days of the British Raj. We were met by a well-dressed and welcoming *bearer* who invited us inside. He lit the kerosene lamps, started a fire in the fireplace, and laid out steaming cups of hot tea and cookies. He then asked what we wanted for dinner. Our beds were freshly made. After a good night of rest and sleep, we awakened to *hazri*. Literally, the *bearer* had brought a pot of hot tea to our bed. Later, he prepared breakfast of boiled eggs, hot flat bread, marmalade, and more hot tea. This brief, idyllic interlude in the remote juniper forests of Baluchistan reflected another and more distant era. Only because of the introduction of air travel in Pakistan were we able to experience such a memorable time with our children.

—

The enormous importance of wheels and transportation in a country like Pakistan was illustrated for us when we lived in Karachi during the late 1980's and early 1990's. Protestors exercised power by calling for a "wheel jam" or strike. Organizers demanded all wheels stop for the day. Streets remained empty, shops closed and the city remained eerily quiet. Although we had heard and read of a "wheel jam" this was our first time to experience it.

We had a problem. We had reservations to leave by plane for a meeting in Nepal. The airport was miles from our home. After deliberating for some time, we decided to venture out. The mission had employed a driver, a young Christian man who was dependable and a good driver. We gathered our bags and hopped in the car with Alex driving. All was well as we sped along the residential area where we lived. However, when we entered a commercial area we were met by a wall of men, ten or twelve rows deep, lining the thoroughfare, shoulder to shoulder. Slowly the car came to a full stop. They gave Alex menacing looks and he was becoming afraid. Several of the young men had large rocks in their hands. They surrounded our car and we waited. One young man, looking as if he might be under the influence of drugs, stared blankly at us. He had a rock in his hand.

I knew that at any minute the rock in his hand might be hurled through our windshield. The tension mounted and after what seemed an eternity, an older man stepped out from the crowd. He told them to move away and the human wall opened up for us to pass. He explained to them that we were foreigners and guests in their country. He waved us on and we sped away, looking at every corner for another blockade. It didn't come.

We managed to reach the airport quickly. There were no other vehicles on the road.

Before leaving, we gave Alex money and instructed him to stay in a hotel located near the airport. We cautioned him to stay off the streets until the "wheel jam" was over. It was a very short distance from the airport to the hotel. Upon our return he told us that rocks had been thrown at him during those few minutes of driving. Thankfully, he was not hurt although the car suffered a few dents.

Thus, we learned the importance of wheels in Pakistan, whether rolling or jammed.

Chapter Three

HOMES

It was called "Sunshine Villa." Built during the later years of British rule, it housed visitors coming to Murree during the summer season. We arrived in late May 1956 and stayed until October, providing an opportunity to start language training. Sunshine Villa became our first home in Pakistan, the place where we lived when we began to learn about the strange new country that we now called home.

Sunshine Villa consisted of a series of three identical apartments strung out like a motel. We lived in the middle apartment. Our neighbors on each side were Anglo-Indian. A retired military officer lived on one side of us. On the other, two women had rented the apartment for the summer. The two Anglo-Indian women were quick to offer advice about how to live in Pakistan. I appreciated their input. The retired military officer kept largely to himself.

Each apartment had a back door. Alongside was an open drain. All the bath and kitchen water emptied into this drain. There was no running water. A water carrier, called a *bihishti*, hauled water in a large goat skin bag strung over his shoulder. Looking for all the world like "Gunga Din," he came twice daily through the back door to fill the large clay pots that supplied us with bath water.

The bathroom was rather large. In the corner, we kept a galvanized tub for bathing. We heated water in the kitchen and carried it to the bathroom. When we finished bathing, we simply turned the tub on its side to empty the water which flowed to the drain outside.

The bathroom also featured an old-fashioned wash stand holding an enamel yellow wash basin trimmed in green. A mirror was hung over the wash stand and, to one side, a large wooden towel rack. A large, clay water pot with an aluminum dipper was placed on the floor next to the wash stand.

The toilet was a square wooden box with a wooden lid. In the seat of the box was a large hole. The seat was removable and a large enamel pot fit perfectly in the frame. Twice each day a cleaner came and emptied the pot, cleaned it, and poured in disinfectant. Somewhere along the way we picked up the name "thunder box" for this very necessary bathroom contraption. The cleaner entered through the back door quietly and left just as unobtrusively. We rarely ever saw the cleaner except on pay day.

Perched on the precipice of the hillside, Sunshine Villa looked toward the majestic Himalayas. A narrow walkway provided access to our front door. An iron railing protected pedestrians from falling. However, we deemed this inadequate and promptly installed chicken wire on the railing to protect David as well as any other toddlers who might be visiting.

Our front door opened right onto this walkway. Below the iron railing was a large open field. Surrounding the field were other houses and apartments for summer visitors, all built in colonial cottage style. Wild flowers bloomed during the summer months and the ground, covered with grass, served as a wonderful playground for children.

We entered our apartment through a small, narrow, and windowless room which we used as a makeshift kitchen. I preferred this arrangement rather than using an outbuilding for cooking, as previous residents had done. I needed more control over our kitchen and didn't much like the idea of going outside in the monsoon rain. We placed a two-burner kerosene cooking stove on wooden boxes. There was no refrigerator. As in the bathroom, we used a large, clay pot to store water. Arranging a table on each side of the room, one for food preparation and the other for washing dishes, I had adequate counter top space. We used two large pans for dish washing.

A screened cabinet served as another essential piece of kitchen equipment. The local word to describe this cabinet and adopted by the British was *dolie*. It reminded us of the kitchen safe our parents and grandparents had used back in rural Georgia. All fresh and perishable foods were kept inside, free from flies or other unwelcome intruders. Each leg of the *dolie* sat in a small container of water kept filled at all times. This prevented ants from accessing our food.

The front room included a wall of glass windows. On the sides, each apartment was separated from the other by a thin wooden partition, leading us to surmise that there had at one time been one long verandah. We often heard conversations from our neighbors, even as they must have heard ours. We lived at close quarters, and the sounds and smells of our neighbors passed easily back and forth. At times, cigarette smoke and garlic wafted through our apartment.

As with the rest of the house, the furnishings in our sitting room were meager: a small two seat sofa; an easy chair; a dining room table with four chairs; a cupboard for dishes; a small book case, and a low table with a lamp. Murree was accustomed to its transitory summer population, and we rented some of these items for a nominal price from a furniture shop in the bazaar.

Our bedroom was directly behind the sitting room. It had no windows, only a door leading to the bathroom. A transom with glass panes, known locally as a *roshandon*, was built in the wall near the ceiling. By pulling on a rope, we could open and close this window for fresh air. Whether opened or closed, it also provided some light into the room during daylight hours. The walls in this room were made of plaster.

The bedroom floor, like all the other floors in the house, was cement. The walls were white washed. We had a *charpai*, a large rope strung bed, rented from the furniture dealer in the Murree bazaar. We also ordered a large mattress filled with fluffed cotton made to fit the bed. Periodically, we hired a local laborer who came to the house and tightened the ropes on the bed whenever it began to sag. If the mattress became too flat, we sent it to the bazaar to get re-fluffed.

Also, we rented a chest of drawers for our clothes. There was no closet. I simply turned a smaller rope-strung bed up on end and placed a pole across the legs, turning an up-ended bed into a rather novel closet. I hung a pretty sheet over the clothes to keep out the dust.

The last piece of furniture needed to complete our home was a collapsible, fold up baby bed, screened on all sides for David. It was one of the last purchases we had made in the United States before leaving for Pakistan. The top lifted and swung back very efficiently. Screened on each side and on top, it served as a protection against mosquitoes. However, once David rolled against the side of the bed while sleeping. Next morning his little arm showed bites all up and down. The mosquitoes had feasted on him through the screen wire. Still, we kept that collapsible travel bed for each of our three children, passing it from one to the other in turn.

I enjoyed decorating our first home in Pakistan. The cane furniture section of the local bazaar in particular was an answer to my dreams. Among other things, I ordered roll-up cane shades for the living room windows. It gave us privacy while also providing a little coziness.

I also wanted a fabric for a softer, lighter touch. In 1956 there was little in the way of draperies to choose from. I had once read in a decorating book that a lot of cheap fabric works better than a little expensive fabric. Browsing around the bazaar one day, some red cotton cloth caught my eye. After measuring the windows, I bought double the width I needed and took it home.

A local tailor came to the house, unfolded his mat on the floor, arranged his hand-turned sewing machine, and sat down. Following my instructions in cutting and sewing up the curtains, they were soon ready. I hung them with suspension wire and hooks. Later, a visitor informed me that the red cotton fabric I had chosen for the windows was the same fabric used by *coolies* to make their turbans. I didn't mind a bit. We simply improvised and made do with what was available locally. Often, we bought a bouquet of fresh flowers from the flower peddler who walked the paths on our mountainside daily. He always smiled cheerfully, the huge basket of flowers balancing precariously atop his head. For our part, we not only filled our home with flowers but also with friends, colleagues—and love.

In October 1956, after seven months of orientation and language training, we moved from the cool mountains surrounding Murree to the dusty plains of Upper Sindh, more than seven hundred miles to the south. We had no idea where we would live but knew that our colleagues had already located and rented a place for us. The little town to which we had been assigned was called Ratodero.

We were met at the Larkana railway station by Ray Buker who had spent his own childhood as the son of Baptist missionaries working in Burma and whose father, also called Ray Buker, had seen us off on the *Steel King* in New York less than six months before. After lunch in Larkana prepared by his wife Jean, Ray drove us eighteen miles over bumpy and dusty desert roads to our new home. He chided me all along the way.

"That's it," he would say, pointing to one mud hut and then another. "That is where you will live,"he would say. I gulped each time he pointed. On the outskirts of Ratodero, we were taken to a large imposing two-storey building. I really had expected to live in a mud house. This one was made of brick. We entered through a very large double wooden door. A narrow brick walkway then led us across a small courtyard. Inside, were three small apartments built wall to wall, rather like condominiums of today. Our colleagues Ralph and Polly Brown and their sons Eddie and Stan occupied one apartment. The first one was used as a visiting place for Ralph and Hu to meet male callers who came to meet the foreigners in this remote corner of Sindh. The third apartment was where we were to live.

Each apartment had its own enclosed courtyard. A covered verandah ran the length of the house. The floors were laid with clay tile. The high walls were very thick and whitewashed. Light was provided through two windows on each side of the door as well as two *roshandans*, near the ceiling to give light. Iron bars affixed to the windows offered some protection. The windows themselves were simple wooden shutters. The first room was large enough and would serve adequately as our living and dining room. Small cupboards had been built in the walls on each side, each with wooden doors. Beyond this room was another room with windows facing outside. We designated this room as our kitchen.

Narrow brick steps led up to a balcony. Wooden cupboards lined the walls. We were told that a wealthy Hindu merchant had once owned the building. The built-in wooden cupboards had been used to house dozens of his Hindu gods.

More narrow stairs led to the bedroom level, consisting of two rooms. All the windows came equipped with bars and wooden shutters.

I loved these windows because they were high off the ground, and we were able keep them open both day and night. We could also have glimpses into the world outside our small, enclosed home.

The second floor included a wide terrace which had multiple uses. It was a wonderful play area for David. I also enjoyed studying in the sun during the short winter months. We slept outside under the stars on this terrace during hot weather, on rope-strung beds equipped with mosquito nets. We appreciated the cool night breeze as well as the opportunity to track the various constellations before we went to sleep.

Toilet facilities were essentially the same as at Sunshine Villa in Murree. Here, too, a *bihishti* hoisting a large goat skin bag on his back brought water to our house each day.

We got busy immediately screening the windows and furnishing our home. Looking through a recent Sears's catalogue and thumbing through the old magazines local craftsmen kept in their shops, we ordered simple yet useful pieces of furniture that could be made according to our specifications. First of all, we ordered a bed. Since none of the local beds came in double size we gave the measurements and ordered one. We also ordered a thick cotton mattress for it. Other pieces of furniture included a settee and two chairs made from rosewood and backed with woven cane, a long low coffee table and two lamp tables, a dining room table and chairs, and two matching chest of drawers, along with a smaller chest for David's clothes. It took several weeks for these custom ordered pieces of furniture to be completed. But we were delighted with the results and used all of them for years, both in Ratodero and in other homes.

We had been told our Ratodero housing arrangement was temporary and negotiations were underway for renting another house. The house, located right in the middle of the little town, was larger and had a well with a pump right in the courtyard. There was a small garden as well.

We looked forward to the move and would go over periodically to check repairs as they were being done. The house had a large verandah and was made of brick. Situated on a narrow brick-paved street, a large double thick wooden door opened into the courtyard. Just inside the courtyard, on the right, and completely separate from the house, was a large room that served as Hu's *otak* where he met with male visitors.

The entrance to our house was on the left and faced a small garden. Across the courtyard was a toilet for visitors and furnished with the usual "thunder box" along with a wooden table, enamel wash basin, towel rack, and a clay pot for water.

The large middle room had a beautiful tile floor and ceiling. The ceilings were very high. Several windows with bars and wooden doors lined the street side of the house and *roshandans* near the ceiling allowed light into the room. Two smaller rooms were located on each side of this great room, one used as a kitchen and the other as a guest bedroom. All three rooms opened onto the verandah. We screened all the windows as well as the verandah. During the winter months, we practically lived on the verandah because the sun was warm and gave a lot of light. Conversely, during the hot weather it was almost impossible to stay on the verandah except during the evenings.

From the courtyard and through a heavy iron door a flight of stairs led to another level with an uncovered terrace and three bedrooms, each one opening onto the terrace. This area was beautiful and functional. There were a couple of small rooms on one end of the terrace. We used one for the toilet with not only one "thunder box" but two-his and hers. We also set up a nice bathroom, installing a long, wide galvanized bath tub with a draining hole and rubber stopper. However, water still had to be hauled up from our hand pump downstairs in the courtyard.

This house in Ratodero was lovely. Stairs led from the bedroom level to a third, rooftop level. It was the highest point in our little town and it seemed as if we could see forever. On the west we could see the outline of the Kirthar Mountains and the distant hills of Baluchistan. On the east we could look toward numerous small villages and the irrigated plains of Sindh. A small, covered brick room, somewhat like a gazebo, had been built on the roof. This, too, provided alternate sleeping space in the hot weather. However, we chose to sleep on the open roof top, using the gazebo to store our bedding during the day.

Ratodero was an electrified town, though electricity only functioned at night. From sun-down to sun-up a single light bulb hung in the center of each room.

Of course, we could not leave the children on the roof alone. I always went to bed early with them. Hu would come along a little later. Each of us had our own *charpai* and mosquito net. We lay in our beds underneath the brilliant sky, discovering the vast dome of constellations, naming them and watching as they wheeled across the Sindh sky. With minimal electricity, there were no bright city lights to mar or obscure the view. If we awakened in the night for any reason, an ever-changing sky was there to greet us. On one of these brilliant nights, we made a special point to track the Soviet-made Sputnik spacecraft on its maiden voyage. We set our clocks so that we could awaken in time to catch this moving satellite glide across the great expanse of sky.

Nights were short during the hot months and, before the sun appeared on the horizon, the air sometimes even became cold. We pulled light blankets over us. It was difficult to leave this zone of cool pure air to head downstairs to face another long hot day.

Leaving the windows and *roshondans* open at night provided some ventilation and allowed cool air to enter. Before the heat of the day became noticeable, we closed them all up in an effort to maintain as much of the coolness as possible. The heat was especially noticeable from noon onwards. Everyone in town took a long rest in the afternoon. We joined them. We did not always sleep. We stayed downstairs where it was much cooler. Sometimes we would get a pillow and lie on the cool tiled floors. With the windows and doors all closed we didn't have much light but we tried to read and study. We filled tubs with water for the children to play in. While Jonathan was still an infant, I remember hiring a little girl in the neighborhood to come and fan him while he napped. We took a lot of showers and drank gallons of iced tea.

Since we would live in this house for the duration of our first four-year term of service, I decided to do some decorating. I enjoyed shopping for local fabrics. There was not much to choose from. However, sometimes I turned bedcovers and table cloths into window treatments. Living in a larger house meant we needed more furniture. We used the verandah a lot, so we furnished it with locally made chairs and seats made from reeds and twine. Large colorful cushions used for sitting on the hard floors were both decorative and functional.

I especially loved pottery. The area in Sindh where we lived was known for its lovely blue and white pottery as well as more earthy brown colors. At times, I even used the utilitarian large clay pots made by local potters effectively. In addition, I found pieces from other parts of the country to brighten and add beauty to our home. I also looked around the countryside for any kind of flowering bush or plant that I could use. Coming across cattails from nearby marshes and plumes from large grasses combined to make lovely arrangements.

I scoured magazines for pictures to frame. I even ordered copies of famous artists that arrived by mail in thin, cardboard tubes. Local framing was cheap. Van Gogh was a personal favorite and for years a copy of his famous "Sunflowers" as well as "The Bridge" decorated our walls. Another favorite, this one by an American artist, was "The Violin." These prints fit well with whatever local art we could find. I tried to blend my past with our present. Over time, I discovered beauty on the backside of a desert.

It was in this very humble home setting that I entertained Begum Nusrat Bhutto, the wife of an up and coming young politician, Zulifkar Ali Bhutto. This was a special event and I wanted everything to be perfect.

I prepared special food for the occasion. Oranges were in season, and I decided to make a gallon of orange ice cream, using an old fashioned crank freezer. It took a long time to cook the custard. When I poured the orange juice into the custard, it curdled. I didn't know at the time that I could freeze it, and it would still turn out perfectly. Instead, I dumped everything out and started again from scratch, deciding this time to make vanilla rather than orange ice cream.

Jean Buker arrived with Mrs. Bhutto from Larkana. Though thoroughly westernized, she was wearing a black *burka* when she entered the courtyard. As soon as the door closed behind her, she yanked it off. I took it from her and hung it on a nearby peg until her departure.

We spent a lovely morning chatting about small things. Through Jean I was to meet Mrs. Bhutto at other times. At one point, she invited me to her lovely California style home in Larkana with a large, kidney shaped swimming pool. I never took to swimming, so I sat on the patio with Mrs. Bhutto while the other women who had been invited swam. She was a lovely, aristocratic woman, somewhat reserved. Her husband later became Foreign Minister and then Prime Minister, electrifying the country with his populist speeches that emphasized the importance of the common man. Years later, he died by hanging when a new military government overthrew him. He and Nusrat had several children and his daughter, Benazir, later became Prime Minister as well. The Bhuttos were a prominent Sindhi family, owning thousands of acres of land. They were well- known figures in the area of Upper Sindh in which we lived. Nusrat traced her origins to Persia while her husband Zulfikar Ali Bhutto represented the Sindhi aristocracy.

—

Another memorable event took place during our years in Ratodero. Earlier, we received a letter from relatives in Macon telling us that Hu's mother had won a contest sponsored by a local television show. Del Ward, the hostess of this very popular noonday show, spotlighting the Middle Georgia area, sought out the mother whose child lived furthest from home. One of Hu's sisters submitted his mother's name. Realistically, it would have been difficult to find anyone at that time and place who had ventured as far from home as we had.

She won the contest. Her prize was a telephone call to her child living on the other side of the planet. We were told to be on the lookout for the phone call.

As it happened, there was exactly one telephone in all of Ratodero. It was located in the post office. Late one night, we heard a knock at our courtyard door. A messenger passed on a note written in English: "Come at once. You have a telephone call from the USSR."

We knew the reference to the USSR was a mistake. Very quickly we dressed, roused the two boys from their deep sleep, and pulled them out of bed and with flashlight in hand made our way through the dimly-lighted narrow streets to the post office. We waited in the semi-dark room for our connection. Then we waited some more. Occasionally, a false ring came through. There was no satellite or even cable connection reaching to Ratodero. Rather, the post office was relying on a radio hook-up. Finally we gave up and walked back home. About a week later we got the message again. Once again, it was late at night. The people living back in Georgia were eating and going about their business and work for the day. We were twelve hours ahead, in the middle of our night, sleepy and tired. Nonetheless, we got up, bundled up the children and walked to the post office.

This time the long distance connection worked. The post office had an extension and I was able to pick up a telephone in another room to join in the conversation. The call was to be limited to three minutes but instead it lasted for about fifteen, much of it marred by the crackle of static. Never in our wildest imagination did we think we would ever be talking to our relatives back in Georgia via telephone. Today such distances are but a cell phone call away.

———

We felt a tinge of sadness when, after four years, we left the house in Ratodero that had become our home. We were departing for the United States and a year of home leave. On our return in June 1961, we were assigned to Shikarpur, a larger town twenty-five miles from Ratodero. Once largely a Hindu town, much of the population had departed for India at partition in 1947. Still, some of the Hindu influences lived on, including the names on local public buildings and in the couple of Hindu temples that still survived.

In the end, we spent more years in Shikarpur than any other town during our years in Pakistan. For our children, Shikarpur will always be home. After living there for a few years, we even gave a name to our home. We called it the *Mehran*, the ancient name for the Indus River that ran through our province of Sindh.

Shikarpur had been a large and flourishing city in years gone by. It was on the trading route to Afghanistan. For years, the town of Kandahar in Afghanistan had a gate known as Shikarpur Gate. On some older maps and globes dating from the nineteenth and early twentieth century, there are often only a couple of cities and towns shown in the area that now constitutes Pakistan. More often than not, one of them is Shikarpur.

The gate leading into Shikarpur's old covered bazaar is called Elephant Gate. At one time, elephants were used as a beast of burden along with the camel caravans that the traders used to connect South Asia with Central Asia. A small caravan *serai* with high mud walls, though crumbling, still survives outside town, a reminder of the time when Shikarpur was filled with the sounds, sights and smells of a great trading center.

Actually, Shikarpur means "hunting place." Long before a town was built, wealthy rulers, landlords, and noblemen hunted wild game in the area. Even today, traces of this hunting tradition live on. On one occasion, a neighbor brought us quail that he had hunted. It was the first time I had ever prepared wild game. Ducks, sometimes migrating from as far away as Siberia, were also hunted down in neighboring marshlands, ending up as a delicacy on many a landlord's table.

During the 1960's, Shikarpur was also included on a different kind of migratory path--that of young European and Americans, referred to as "hippies," traveling from West to East. Buses going from Nepal to Europe sometimes stopped in Shikarpur for refueling and rest stops. Hu on occasion met some of these travelers in the bazaar, startling encounters that reflected the fact that the world really was becoming smaller. We provided a room and food for some of them a number of times. Not all of them were drug users; many were young people who simply wanted to see the world.

We were pleased about our new assignment to Shikarpur. Once again, we lived in a temporary house while waiting for ours to get repaired and renovated. This temporary house was known as the "Boy Scout Bungalow," presumably because it had once served as a meeting place for boys participating in the local scouting organization.

When we first saw the big brick house we had been assigned, we wondered how we could possibly ever make a home out of it. It was considered evacuee property, having been owned by a wealthy Hindu who had fled to India in 1947. Simultaneously, many Muslims had fled from India to Pakistan, leaving properties behind. Hindus, who fled what is now Pakistan were to be given property of equal value in India, while Muslims who fled India were to be given property of equal value in Pakistan. Much of the property lay unclaimed for years. Even when new owners claimed property, they often did not want to live in the place.

The particular house where we were to live was at one time located on the outskirts of town. In fact, it had been built as an entertainment hall. It was a fairly large one story building, beautifully built with imported tile floors and colored glass window panes and mirrors. Teak wood was used for doors and windows throughout, often involving beautiful inlay and intricate carved designs. However, we knew immediately that extensive repairs and renovations would be needed to make it livable. Fortunately, the mission was able to purchase the property, and the repair work proved to be a good investment.

The main room was large with doors and windows taking up most of the wall space. A verandah with high archways wrapped around the house on three sides. Three small rooms ran across the back of the house to complete the structure. Outside were several small rooms in the courtyard which had been used as quarters for servants. Near the street and the entrance to the courtyard were a couple of other rooms, one of which served as a reception room for male guests. A small garden had been laid out with a walkway at the front of the house, which was surrounded by a tiled terrace.

The structure was very much showing its age following years of neglect. The thick mud walls were beginning to erode. Still, we were able to restore the central room into a large living area. We then turned the back rooms into two bedrooms and a kitchen. Just outside the back door, we built a small bathroom with a shower and our first flush toilet in Pakistan. In fact, I believe it was the very first flush toilet ever to be built in Shikarpur. Hu ordered plans for building a septic tank from the States and, step by step, directed a mason in building it.

We had a hand pump in the yard but no way to move the water to the bathroom. Therefore, we built a platform outside the bathroom, installing one of the large steel barrels we had used to ship goods from the United States as a water tank. The water carrier kept the barrel full by using a small ladder to reach the top. There was no need to heat the water in the summer. During the winter months, we built a small fire under the barrel to heat the water. While still essentially an outhouse, the installation of a flush toilet and shower made us feel like we had truly arrived. Later, we installed an electric pump to move the water. We also put into place a custom built, chipped marble bathtub.

After living in the *Mehran* for a few years we made other renovations. For example, we closed off portions of the verandah and in this way added two more bedrooms and an office/study for Hu. We also added a kitchen and built cabinets using wood from our shipping crates, painting the cabinets a marine blue. Still later, I got a kitchen sink and installed plumbing to pipe in water. During the early years, we used a kerosene stove and kerosene refrigerator. Some years later, the Canadians built a thermal power plant on the Indus River, providing much more reliable electricity to Upper Sindh. We then upgraded to an electric refrigerator. Bottled gas became available; making the smelly and unreliable kerosene stove a thing of the past. Remarkably, a Pakistani friend asked to buy the stove and then used a local craftsman to convert it to gas. When we finally left Pakistan in 1993, the stove was still being used in her apartment in Karachi where she had retired after many years of living in Shikarpur.

Decorating the living room with high ceilings and making it into a cozy livable place to relax and entertain became a challenge. I often sat in the large room just looking around for inspiration. I counted nine big beautiful double teak wood doors as well as six teak wood windows and six teak wood cupboards that had been built into the wall. The wall space between these windows, doors and cupboards was limited.

I made a big decision. I would cover most of the doors and all the windows with draperies. This was a gigantic task. The ceilings were at least fifteen feet high with *roshandans* near the top on each wall. I traveled to Karachi to look for drapery material, specifically seeking an indigenous rather than Western design.

I also decided to color the white-washed walls. The local painter was amazed at my choice: I called it beige and he called it dirt! He had never seen a wall painted dirt color before. I stuck to my ideas. After all, I reasoned, a beige color would unlikely show dust.

The drapery fabric I found in Karachi had the same color background as the walls. An indigenous design had been printed on the fabric, a Mogul wine decanter, tall, thin and graceful. I do not recall how many yards of cloth I bought, but it was sufficient to go above the highest door and fall to the floor and covered most of the windows and doors.

These would be the first real draperies I had ever made. My research included going through decorating books I had brought from the US. I went to work using a sewing machine given to me by my mother-in-law out of her first "old age" pension check. By the time I finished the sewing and hemming, the carpenter had finished installing the holders and long wooden rods on which to hang them.

It was amazing what those draperies did, not only for the acoustics but also in providing a welcome backdrop for a warm and cozy living area. The Georgia pine bookcases we had used as a shipping crate became a room divider. The huge room had been turned into a comfortable place for family living.

We also made a large dining room table as well as a buffet and china cabinet. Our ministry of hospitality grew, and we were able to entertain our guests with ease. Just as this structure had originally been built as an entertainment hall, we were now using it to entertain our guests who came from far and wide. Sometimes now I sit down and look through the guest books that I kept over many years. I enjoy recalling the names of those who graced our home with their presence. They came from every corner of the world as well as from every area of our town and country.

One of the guests was Sir Henry Holland, a well-known eye surgeon from England who spent his life in a remote part of Pakistan giving sight to thousands of people. He founded a hospital in Quetta that continues to exist to this day. Most of the patients trekked to the hospital from the remote mountainous and desert areas of Baluchistan and Sindh; others traveled from as far away as neighboring Afghanistan.

It was my honor and privilege to bake a delicious pineapple chiffon cake for Sir Henry's ninetieth birthday celebration. We gathered with his family and close friends in Shikarpur, celebrating a life that stretched back to his birth in the north of England in February 1875.

These celebrations also served as a fitting way to inaugurate our new set of dishes. On a recent trip to Karachi, Hu had decided it was time to replace our thick melamine dishes with real china. He came home with a beautiful set of imported dinnerware made in Czechoslovakia. White and translucent, each piece was decorated with tiny pink flowers, green leaves and gold trimmed. The edges were delicately scalloped. The set came in a service for eight plus a complete coffee set with demitasse cups and saucers, a lovely teapot, fruit bowl, covered serving pieces and a large platter.

The new dinner set served as our combined birthday, Christmas, and anniversary present to each other for the year. Years later, as I write these words, I am looking at the coffee pot and a cup and saucer I have kept through the years, a reminder of the many people and events that have enriched our lives.

The size of our living space in Shikarpur meant that we had to obtain additional furniture as well. In those years, local crafts were much more affordable than today. A very large brass table, placed on four pronged legs carved from a single piece of rosewood fit perfectly. We also purchased a large floor covering, a *dhurrie*. In fact, we purchased this item at a district jail where inmates made and sold handicrafts to help defray the cost of running the institution. The *dhurrie,* together with the brass table, provided a beautiful completion to our newly decorated room.

Once, on home leave, I mentioned to a friend how difficult it was to keep green plants in the hot climate. I loved having plants in the house. Soon afterwards, I received a telephone call from the Greyhound bus station informing me that a parcel had arrived. I had no idea a parcel was coming. We hastily drove down to the bus depot to pick up a very long, brown box. Opening it, we pulled back the green florist paper and discovered a large rubber plant, long stemmed yellow daffodils, white Easter lilies and still more greenery. They looked so real. The Easter lilies even had a tiny bruised spot. They were all artificial, probably some of the first to become available. I took them back to Pakistan and for years they added pleasure and beauty to our home. Later silk flowers became available and I made good use of them as well.

Brick steps outside our house led upstairs to a large roof. As in Ratodero, we used the roof for outside sleeping during the hot weather. When our children were small, we also used the roof top as an additional play area. Our downstairs yard was small and did not have enough room to spread out toys. However, the flat roof was spacious and safe, providing a warm and sunny space to play during the winter months.

We hauled sand up for a sandbox. David had a Matchbox fleet of cars and trucks. Jonathan delighted in playing with his toy soldiers. On occasion, the boys even rode their bicycles up on the roof. Nancy had her very own playhouse, built from the local reeds and straw used by poor people to build their homes. She decorated it and had tea parties for her dolls. Our pet poodle Dixie also loved lying around in the sun on the roof with the children.

The several outside rooms surrounding the courtyard provided additional space for projects involving the children. One year, David became a "Mad Scientist," hanging a sign above the door to identify himself as such. He had been given a chemistry set for Christmas and was thrilled to have his own lab. We had no idea what kind of experiments he carried out.

One day we heard a loud boom that sounded like an explosion.

"David, David," yelled Baroo, our household help.

He ran to the room where David had set up his laboratory. In fact, we all ran, scared to death about what we might find. David opened the door, surprised at all the hoopla and aggravated by the interruption. He was hard at work but nothing had gone awry. A tire repair shop was located next door and a tire had blown up while being filled with air. We were all very relieved.

The renovations gave each of the children their own room as they grew up. Since they went to boarding during the school year and lived dormitory style with a number of other children, we wanted to give them their own private space when they lived at home in Shikarpur during their three months of winter holidays. We encouraged them to express themselves, and they enjoyed fixing up their rooms with their collectibles, often including locally made toys and various artifacts.

All of us enjoyed our time in Shikarpur. We lived there for twelve years, the longest time we had stayed in one place. When it was time to leave, there was more than a little sadness as we said our final good-byes.

—

The next move, in 1973, was to Hyderabad, a much larger city more than one hundred miles to the south. It was located on the Indus River and, before the arrival of the British, had served as the capital of Sindh. Parts of the old fort built by the Talpurs still stood. The battle of Miani, in which the British had defeated the Talpurs, had taken place in the forests along the Indus River, north of Hyderabad.

Hyderabad was a city of both history and rich culture. It was also a commercial center as well as a transportation juncture for roads and railway tracks leading to other areas of Sindh, including Karachi to the south, Sukkur to the north and Mirpurkhas and the border with India to the east. The town boasted industry, museums, and a leading university, other well known educational institutions, and a large irrigation barrage across the Indus River regulating the water flow to the farming areas. A small community of other foreigners also lived in Hyderabad, and I had relatively more freedom living there than I did living deeper in the interior of Sindh.

Finding suitable housing was a challenge. We finally located a newly-built bungalow that had not yet been hooked up for electricity. The red tape required to obtain power and a telephone during the early 1970s was formidable, requiring long hours and endless delays. However, it was all worth it the day the movers pulled into the courtyard of our brand new home.

It seemed as if we really were entering the modern age. The floors were made of marble, and plenty of glass windows, all with iron grates. The house itself was only one storey and built of reinforced concrete. The roof was flat, but unlike in Shikarpur or Ratodero, could not be used for sleeping. The wall that surrounded the house was much lower than the ones we were used to. The comparative openness as well as the lows walls made me uneasy.

Our Hyderabad home had three bedrooms, each with attached modern baths. The guest bedroom was just off the entrance. We designated this room as Hu's office space and meeting room. All the rooms were connected by a long hallway with windows that let in plenty of light. The kitchen was spacious and included a second "keeping room" for washing dishes and sorting fresh produce. Natural gas had been discovered in Pakistan in the intervening years, and big cities like Hyderabad were now connected to the national gas grid. I was thrilled to finally have a modern stove. Electricity, too, was more dependable than ever before. We had fans and, for the first time ever, an air conditioner.

David had graduated from high school and moved to the United States to begin his college years. Jonathan squeezed into the office/guest room for the short time he was home. Our youngest, Nancy, had a beautiful room she enjoyed during the winter breaks. International businesses were beginning to locate in Hyderabad, and she was able to get a paying job as a typist in one of them. Muslim women had not yet joined the workforce in large numbers and a young woman working in an office raised a few eyebrows.

The office where Nancy worked was near our home. Her American boss was aware of the cultural nuances. He watched over Nancy like a father. She was a teenager and a beautiful one at that. Her dark hair was long. Her big brown eyes were expressive. And she had the same olive complexion as a Pakistani.

Nancy made friends with some local girls and enjoyed her time at home. Although Hyderabad was a larger city and some of the restraints of living in a country that remained largely segregated by gender might have been lessened, she still did not have the freedom of going out alone. One of us always accompanied her. She always wore the Pakistani dress; *shalwar, kameez* and *duputta*. A couple of times we noticed young male college students following us to find out where we lived. Occasionally, one or the other of them would ride by on their motorcycles or drive by in their cars for a closer look.

Modern conveniences such as gas, dependable electricity and an easier-to- keep, smaller house meant I no longer had to hire full time household help, an expense that we could in any case hardly afford. Instead, I turned to part-time help, hiring a local Christian girl to come a couple of days a week.

We continued to offer hospitality, and our home became a meeting place for work as well as socializing.

The house in Hyderabad included a patio. We put a swing there and enjoyed the cool evenings with wind blowing from across the Indus River nearby. Now and then, I would pack a small basket with a thermos of tea and a box of cookies. We walked together across an open field to the banks of the Indus and watched the sunset, the light still illuminating the few fishermen and boats on the river until the first stars began to appear. It was a relaxing way to end a busy day.

Across the street from our house was a mental hospital, known locally as the *pagal khana* or "crazy house." We did not like the term. However, at times we had to use it when giving directions. The hospital was a landmark everyone recognized.

Sometimes, late at night, I heard the screams of a woman from across the wall. The patients represented various degrees of mental illness. Some probably did not need to be there at all. However, in the absence of relatives, there was no other place for them to go.

I had the opportunity to visit the hospital. On a visit to the mother of a friend, I went straight to the office and gave my name and reason for coming. While walking down the hall, I met a lovely woman, not very old, with regal bearing. She spoke in a loud voice and wore tattered clothes. I began to speak with her in Sindhi. However, she responded to me in the Queen's English. Shortly, I found the person I had come to meet. She was a tiny, frail little woman, curled up in her bed. She did not know English and we conversed in Sindhi. I had brought her some sweets. After a while, I left her to return to the office. The woman, who had spoken to me in excellent English, saw me, waved her scarf and invited me back. In retrospect, I wished that I had followed up on her offer and gotten her story. It must have been an interesting if tragic one.

We lived for several years in Hyderabad and then returned for an extended period to the United States, enough time for all three of our children to graduate from college and enter into the early years of their careers.

—

When we returned to Pakistan six years later, in 1984, it was to Karachi, Pakistan's largest and most dynamic city with a population which by that time had increased to well over ten million people. A few parts of the city were as modern as any in the rapidly developing East Asian countries such as Malaysia and Singapore. Other sections were more like Kipling's "city of dreadful night," populated by millions of poor migrants from the interior of Pakistan seeking their fortunes in a teeming metropolis that served as Pakistan's main port and commercial center.

We lived in three different houses during our years in Karachi, which also proved to be our final years in Pakistan. The first house was small but suitable for the two of us and our work. It was a low, L-shaped cement building with a carport and a small garden. There was a long living and dining area, small kitchen, glass enclosed verandah and three bedrooms with attached baths. As always, we turned one of the bedrooms into Hu's workroom/study. Another served as a guest room and the third became the master bedroom, which was air-conditioned.

It was about this time that a number of expatriates prevailed upon us to begin an English-speaking international church. Some had worked elsewhere overseas where such a church had developed and felt strongly that Karachi should have one as well. With some trepidation, we allowed ourselves to become involved. What began in our modest living room with three couples and a borrowed piano keyboard rather quickly became the International Church of Karachi, involving many dozens of worshippers. The congregation met each Friday, the weekly holiday then observed across Pakistan. Hu became the volunteer pastor and others participated in leadership positions. Over time, the church emerged as an important institution within the broader international community. During times of crisis and tragedy the church provided comfort and solace. For example, Hu provided comfort to the community when a Pan American jet on the tarmac of Karachi airport was hijacked in September of 1986, leaving dozens dead or injured.

As the size of the international congregation grew, we had to move to a second, somewhat larger house. This one was two levels and included a large yard. In effect, the downstairs served as the church and housed Hu's office while the upstairs became our home. Once again, the house had lovely marble floors. The kitchen countertops were also made of marble. A large hallway upstairs served as our sitting room, a small cozy nook for reading, music for the very first time we had a TV.

While living in this house, we were visited by an intruder. Contrary to what others did, I locked our bedroom door when we went to bed. During the night, I was awakened by the sound of our door knob being turned. I raised my head, listening intently for the sound to return. The dogs next door were barking loudly. The door remained silent so I turned over and went back to sleep.

Hu got up early the next morning for his daily run along the Arabian Sea. On returning, he noticed the TV was missing and called for me to come quickly. I jumped up, and we found our house had been ransacked. Every room upstairs had been trashed. The office where we kept a rather large steel safe for valuables had been tampered with.

We called the police who came and did some investigation. Tracks lead to our high wall over which the thieves most likely had entered and left. Further investigation showed that the house had been entered through the kitchen door. Although the door was locked securely, the thief had opened a window near the door, reached in and unlocked the door. A screen door had been cut to open the door. It was unnerving. We learned that a series of burglaries had occurred throughout the city during the night, most of them more serious than the one at our home.

This house sported a tiled roof, a new trend in Karachi at the time. For the first time, we also had a large garden, big enough to host outdoor activities. We bought a very old croquet set. It was much larger than a regular one and had come from the prestigious Sindh Club where in colonial times the British *sahibs* enjoyed their evening sports. We enjoyed an evening of croquet once in a while. Church functions were also held on the spacious lawn. It was easy to rent a tent for special events held at Christmas, Easter and other times. The church continued to grow in numbers, and the house seemed to shrink. Once again it was time to look for larger facilities.

A larger house but smaller yard became available. We found ourselves moving again. This house was more easily divided into separate sections.We enjoyed a very private apartment at the back of the house. These large bungalows were designed for joint families where sons and their families lived with their father and mother. This one was ideal. The front part of the house had a large living/dining area and a large foyer which became the sanctuary. The front bedroom served as church office. Upstairs there were two large bedrooms and bath with a large hallway and a roof top the size of the entire floor space downstairs. These rooms provided Sunday school rooms, and the roof top became an excellent accommodation for church events. As in the previous house, it was easy and cheap enough to rent a tent to cover the entire area for special occasions. The church congregation assumed financial responsibility for their share of rent and utilities.

Downstairs and halfway through the house were glass doors that led to another area which served as our private apartment. A small hallway became our dining room. The modern kitchen was sheer luxury for me. The counter tops were marble. Attached to the kitchen was a smaller kitchen, complete with a table top stove, sink and built in cabinets. These houses, built for large extended families, catered to their life style. This kitchen was regarded as the "dirty kitchen," meaning that all the cleaning of vegetables and meat as well as food preparation took place in this area.

I turned the "dirty kitchen" into my private water purification plant. We had city water flowing into an underground tank, below the carport. One look into the tank convinced me never to drink water unless I knew the source. Cockroaches by the thousands found refuge in the damp, dark underground. The tank was never full of water. Rather, there were water shortages, and we often had to buy water from water trucks that prowled the streets of our neighborhood. These large tankers delivered water to the underground tank, from where it would be electrically pumped to a second tank on the roof. From there, gravity took over and every tap and bathroom in the house received water. When the water finally reached the "dirty kitchen," I filled large metal pots that went directly on the stove for boiling. I timed the boiling myself to ensure a full twenty minutes at boiling point.

I jealously guarded our water supply because I firmly believed most diseases were water-borne and could be avoided. After cooling overnight, the boiled water went directly to a water purification system consisting of four ceramic filters fitting inside a container that in turn fit inside another larger stainless steel container, out of which flowed pure clean water, suitable for drinking.

The process of boiling water became a daily process, especially before the arrival of the weekly church crowd. With tongue in cheek, I sometimes referred to my job description as running a water purification plant. Every ice cube, every gallon of tea, every glass of cold water, every cup of tea or coffee, all the water for cleaning fruits and vegetables, and any recipe requiring water came from this system.

The small hallway we used for a dining room was easy to decorate. I asked a young American woman to stencil the upper part of the wall. A lovely light fixture hung over the oval, light wood table. The modern dining chairs were padded. There was room for a narrow sideboard over which I hung a mirror. The mirror gave a feeling of spaciousness.

To the side of this small room was a bedroom with adjacent bath. As a guest room, it was frequently occupied.

The dining room flowed into a small living area. It was just large enough for a sofa, some comfortable chairs and tables with lamps. A very large window with iron grill work looked out upon a terrace and garden and the back wall. Here in the U.S. I still use the Oriental rug, a table and rocking chair that furnished the small room. The pictures and art work that once hung on our walls in Karachi now adorn our modest retirement home in Macon, Georgia, near the place where I grew up.

This third house in Karachi—and our final home in Pakistan—also included two bedrooms, each with a separate bath. The smaller one served as Hu's office and the larger one became our bedroom. A large window looked out on the garden.

The bedroom was large enough for two easy chairs and a television set. The garden was small but lovely, featuring many tropical plants. Bougainvillea was easy to grow and the walls were covered with gorgeous shades of pink. Hibiscus bloomed and poinsettia burst forth with red blooms in time for the Christmas season. The sweet smelling *rat-ki-rani*, queen of the night, added its soft pungent fragrance permeating the evenings whenever we had a chance to sit outside. Once I discovered a small cobra in the garden. Hearing me screaming to the top of my voice, the gardener came running. He located the snake and removed it from the garden. From that time, I kept a watchful eye out for snakes.

Since early childhood, I have heard the phase "Be it ever so humble, there is no place like home." I have lived in many homes throughout my life, some of them decidedly humble and others more spacious and prepossessing. No matter where I have lived, I nearly always repeat that phrase when returning home from a long trip or even a day or two away. It is the truth. At the end of the day and despite having traveled across many parts of the world, I am a homebody at heart, perfectly happy with being at home, wherever that might be.

Chapter Four

FOOD

On our first voyage across the Atlantic on the *Steel King*, I dreamed of food. The dream stayed with me and recurred on more than a few occasions during our first few months in Pakistan.

We had spent five weeks on the high seas from New York to Karachi. I loved every minute of it. We ate with the officers in the dining room. The heavy steel tables attached to the floor did not move, even when the seas became rough. The food, more suited to a working ship's crew than gourmet, was excellent. We looked forward to every meal. Eating was our favorite activity on board ship. Perhaps this is the reason why, after the gentle rocking of the ship had lulled me to sleep, I dreamed of food.

The principle theme of my dream was a large super market waiting for me when I arrived in Pakistan, just like the supermarkets that I was familiar with back in Macon, Georgia. It had everything I wanted. I would lack for nothing.

Thoughts of this dream lingered for awhile. Upon our arrival at the hill station of Murree to begin language study, our colleagues prepared our first meal. The table was set with a lovely cloth and fresh flowers. There was a roast, mashed potatoes, gravy, English peas, carrots, homemade rolls, butter, and apple pie with a mound of whipped cream for dessert.

The home was warm and cozy and the menu was mouth-watering. However, already tired and a little sick from the long train journey north, there was a psychological barrier I just couldn't cross: major portions of our meal, including the snow white butter and cream and the choice tenderloin, came from a domesticated water buffalo.

I had seen herds of these strange creatures, large, black, and big-boned, from our train window. Often, they were cooling themselves in a canal, walking beside the railway track, or ambling down some dusty village road.

With images of living water buffaloes filling my mind, I nearly choked on every bite. Somehow, I managed to eat a respectable amount of the food set before us. We thanked our hosts, Ralph and Polly Brown, profusely and went home to our small apartment at Sunshine Villa. Walking back, we pondered the food challenges that might lie ahead.

Not long afterward, we were introduced to a man, Saeed, who was to be our helper. We were told that he was a cook. Everyone had a cook. It was the custom. Many had worked for British households during the colonial period. Our colleagues had already employed cooks. Now, they had arranged one for us as part of our orientation to daily living in Pakistan.

Although our new cook spoke very little English, we somehow managed to communicate. He arranged to have milk delivered to our door daily. The deliveryman arrived early in the morning with two large milk cans anchored on each side of his bicycle. Using a long-handled dipper, he measured out our daily requirement.

We bought milk by the *seer*, measuring roughly two pounds. The milk was poured through a white cheese cloth tied across an aluminum pot, a technique which helped strain out dirt and other debris. The pot was taken immediately to our kerosene stove and boiled for at least twenty minutes to kill any germs. It was then set aside for cooling. Usually, we let it cool overnight. By the next morning, we were able to use a slotted spoon to remove a thick layer of white cream. This was put aside for making homemade butter as well as fresh cream to top off our desserts.

I asked our new cook to bring meat, potatoes, and vegetables from the local market. I wanted him to duplicate that first dinner we had been served on our arrival. However, when he returned from shopping, I took one look at the meat and became sick.

Let me be clear. I had grown up on a farm in rural Middle Georgia, surrounded by domesticated animals. I had seen cows and hogs butchered. I had watched while my mother killed and dressed chickens. I was not a wimp. But, when I saw the dark color of the dead flesh and got a whiff of a freshly slaughtered chunk of meat, I knew I had a problem.

Nonetheless, I asked Saeed to cook the meat. When we sat down for dinner, the meat was so tough that we could not even cut it. I was glad. If we couldn't cut it, we wouldn't have to eat it. We enjoyed a vegetable dinner instead.

The fact that the government imposed two meatless days each week helped me to avoid eating meat. This measure was introduced for economic reasons, the idea being that if people ate less meat, families would save money and the herds of cattle would grow faster. Very probably the idea had been introduced by the British government during World War II, when commodities of all types were in short supply.

I didn't mind at all. On meatless days, we simply ate vegetables, often supplemented by eggs, boiled egg curry and creamed eggs on toast.

As the days turned into weeks, I made a greater effort to incorporate meat into our diet. However, the reality was that I kept on rejecting the meat every time the cook brought it into our kitchen. I would not even try to cook it. I just gave it back to Saeed and we continued to eat vegetables.

Chicken and lamb were also available. These were the most expensive meats available in Pakistan at the time and most people ate them only on special occasions. I thought if we could find a chicken, I could possibly cook it and serve it to the family.

I asked the cook to buy a chicken. When he returned from the bazaar, I took one look at the scrawny live fowl with black feathers that he called a chicken and shuddered. Even the skin under the black feathers was dark.

We had been told that sick chickens often found their way to the market. As a precaution, we should always observe the chicken for some time before butchering it. We put the chicken, with its legs tied together, in a small open box. My spirits fell. Every time I passed the chicken box, I became more agitated and depressed.

"Perhaps," I thought, "this is not a chicken after all; it is a crow or some other strange kind of Pakistani bird."

David, running around the apartment, must have been aware of my emotional state. He was very interested in the box and kept looking at the strange bird inside. At one point, I went to the bedroom and knelt beside my bed to pray.

"Lord," I cried in my despair. "Give me some indication that this is indeed a chicken. As a sign, please let this bird, if it is a chicken, cackle."

Half-heartedly, I tried to return to my language study. Language learning was difficult enough. However, at this point it was my inability to deal with the food issue in Pakistan that threatened to send us home prematurely.

Thankfully, my feelings of depression and catastrophe were interrupted when David ran to me, shouting.

"Mommy, mommy," he said. "Praise the Lord—the chicken is cackling!"

I jumped from my chair and joined him in praise for this unusual answer to an unusual prayer. Saeed killed and dressed the chicken and I cooked it. It may have cackled, but it was still inedible.

—

For a time, I resorted to other measures. A general store called Essajee & Sons had opened on the Murree Mall, stocking various imported food items, all of them expensive. I bought a box of stale American Kellogg corn flakes, all that I could afford. On another occasion, I found peaches at the local market. They were delicious—until I noticed a large white worm crawling out of one of them.

As my awful food experience continued, I realized Saeed was not actually a cook at all. By this time, I had learned enough from others to know that well qualified cooks who spoke some English were in fact available. We let Saeed go and then hired Zardad Khan. His English was quite decipherable, he worked well in the kitchen, and he knew how to shop in the marketplace. His *chits* indicated long tenures with British officials and he came highly recommended.

It is no exaggeration to say that Zardad saved my life in Pakistan. Slowly, he introduced us to his repertoire of English dishes. He knew how to take tough cuts of buffalo and tenderize them with locally grown papaya. He shopped for well-fed fowl that looked, cackled, and tasted like chicken. Even though he was mostly illiterate, he was able to follow recipes. Over the years he learned to cook American food as well.

I taught Zardad everything I knew, including how to make a lemon meringue pie. To this day I cannot produce a lemon meringue pie as wonderful as his. He also learned to use yeast and became an expert at baking bread, dinner rolls, cinnamon rolls, and doughnuts. He made potato chips, producing the thinnest, tastiest potato chips I have ever eaten.

Times changed in Pakistan and more diplomats, businessmen, and other expatriates arrived. We could not possibly compete with the higher wages they offered. In the end, when Pakistan's capital moved from Karachi to Rawalpindi and then Islamabad, we lost Zardad to the Italian Ambassador. Later I heard that the ambassador was so impressed with Zardad's skills that he took him on subsequent assignments.

Many years later, we met Zardad on the streets of Murree, after he had returned from one of his several postings with the Italian Ambassador abroad. He insisted on coming to our home to cook dinner for us. We enjoyed a delicious dinner that finished with a perfect lemon meringue pie.

The dream I had on the *Steel King* of an American-style supermarket in Pakistan became much less visionary as I became more familiar with local food markets and how they worked.

In fact, the food bazaar ranked among the most colorful and interesting places in Pakistan. Seasonal fruits were carefully arranged and always looked appetizing. Baskets of dried fruits and nuts were stacked together, including walnuts, raisins, apricots, figs, dates, currants, and pistachios. Usually, the mounds of colorful spices sent me into a sneezing frenzy. Whole wheat as well as unbleached white flour always seemed plentiful. Huge bags of rice sat on the ground, including the scented *basmati* variety for which Pakistan has since become famous. Imported white sugar was available but rationed. When this was out of stock, we had to settle for local brown sugar, which was often lumpy and dirty.

Over time, I realized virtually everything we needed for food was available in some form or another in the local bazaar. I also realized the necessity to have a local cook who was a professional in his own right. In fact, hiring a cook trained by the British was possibly the smartest thing we ever did, at least as far as feeding the family and preserving our health is concerned.

Among other things, Zardad introduced us to aspects of an expatriate culture that extended to British times. For example, we still maintain the custom of stopping for a morning and afternoon cup of tea. Over time, such breaks came to be seen as almost essential, providing an important time-out in the midst of extreme heat and long days. Our Pakistani friends also practiced this custom inherited from the British Raj.

After losing Zardad to the Italian ambassador, I was very lucky. We found another cook, Yakoob. Just as Zardad had been trained by the British, so was Yakoob. I taught him how to prepare American foods, even as he introduced me to British recipes. He was especially good in preparing meats of all types. He knew which cuts were most tender for steaks, roasts, and insisted on grinding our own hamburger meat. He was very competent, not only in the kitchen but also in the market place.

Since Pakistan was a Muslim country, we never ate pork unless gifted a can of ham, bacon or hotdogs by an expatriate traveler passing through town or a diplomat who had access to an Embassy commissary. Spiced beef became our alternative to ham at Christmas. It took about a week to marinate in a special spicy solution containing salt petre; it also involved daily turning and pricking with a fork. Afterwards, it was cooked slowly until it could be thinly sliced like ham.

Yakoob not only introduced spiced beef to our diet. He prepared a variety of other meat dishes, including beef Wellington, Yorkshire pudding, beef stroganoff, roast lamb with mint sauce, lamb chops and filet mignon. Of course, these dishes were reserved for special occasions. But, despite my concerns during those first miserable weeks in Pakistan, we ate well and rarely lacked for anything good as far as food was concerned.

While we spent our summers in Murree learning Sindhi and Urdu, it was during those months I also learned how to run a household. This knowledge provided the foundation for what proved to be thirty-four happy years in Pakistan. The missionary community that gravitated toward Murree during the summer months was quite large and came from many countries, including England, Scotland, Germany, Australia, New Zealand, Sweden, Norway, Canada and the United States. A number of those within this diverse group had served in pre-partition British India, bringing with them a wealth of experience in how to cope. The old timers regarded us as young whippersnappers and perhaps we were. Certainly, I learned much from these early encounters, including a sense for how the British approached life while living abroad. They were sociable and we relished every dinner invitation we received from them.

On one occasion when we were invited to dinner, I saw a small glass dish of yellow mustard—the first I'd seen since leaving America. I could hardly wait to spread some on the meat. Suddenly, I learned the difference between English mustard and American mustard: horseradish!

Becoming more secure in planning and preparing food, we began to invite friends over for lunch or dinner. It was now my turn to introduce friends and colleagues to new varieties of food. In my case, that meant old time Southern cooking. Local produce and fruit was adaptable. I managed to find a vanilla wafer substitute for making delicious banana puddings. On occasion I served fried onion rings as well as chicken barbecue baked in a kerosene oven. Although hot tea is ever-present in Pakistan, our particular contribution was to introduce iced tea, Southern style.

One Sunday after church we invited friends for dinner. This was a popular time to entertain as all of us were busy during the week in language study.

A few days earlier, I had found fresh corn in the market and I couldn't wait to boil some for dinner. We enjoyed a sumptuous meal. I didn't notice that the boiled corn was missing from the table. We finished the main course and cleared the table for dessert, anticipating the banana pudding. Imagine my surprise when our cook brought in a platter of boiled corn. Apparently, he had learned from a former employer that this was the way it was done. I was speechless. I adopted a number of new food customs that summer, but this one I did not.

If food availability was one early concern, food preparation presented challenges of an entirely different kind. Every drop of water used in the kitchen had to be boiled. Similarly, we could not eat raw fruits and vegetables without scrubbing them with soap and water, soaking them in disinfectant and then rinsing them in boiled water.

My kitchen rule was whatever could be peeled after a thorough wash was safe to eat. Staples such as rice, flour and cereal had to be checked for beetles. I also had to take brown sugar, clean it and then boil it down. After straining it through a cheese cloth, it made delicious syrup which tasted good on cereal as well as for cooking. Dried fruits and nuts were always available but always required thorough cleaning.

We were very pleasantly surprised to find a wide variety of fruits and vegetables. They were seasonal, of course. When available, we ate eggplant, okra, cauliflower, spinach, tomatoes, onions, sweet peas and carrots. We relished familiar fruits such as apples, peaches, pears, and bananas as well as the more exotic ones, including mango, guava, pomegranates, and dates. Citrus fruits of all kinds—grapefruit, oranges, tangerines, *kinu*, lemons, and limes were available in abundance. Melons were produced locally and very sweet. Some of the best were imported from Afghanistan.

By the time we left Pakistan, missionaries, aid workers, and local entrepreneurs had introduced an entirely new set of other fruits and vegetables to urban markets throughout Pakistan, such as strawberries, broccoli, and asparagus. Punjab province in particular is incredibly fertile and virtually everything planted somehow seems to grow there.

Holidays such as Thanksgiving and Christmas stirred a longing for traditional American foods. I literally spent weeks getting dried fruits and nuts ready for our Christmas fruit cake. Cleaning the raisins and sometimes dates by soaking them to loosen the dirt took a very long time. I even learned how to candy citrus peel. Despite the hard work, the finished product was always well worth the effort.

One Thanksgiving I developed a strong hunger for sweet potato pie. There were no sweet potatoes available, but somehow I came up with the idea that carrots might work instead. Why not carrots? After all, they were golden in color, sweet and delicious. I looked through my cookbooks and pulled out a recipe for sweet potato pie. All the spices listed in the cookbook were available—and, yes, our Thanksgiving dinner included sweet potato pie made out of carrots!

I have said I never found sweet potatoes locally available during the years I lived in Pakistan. In fact, I did eventually come across a white potato that locals called sweet. Local vendors pushed around a cart with them baking in hot coals. They were very popular during the short winter months. I had never seen them before so we bought some. We baked them as we wanted to try to see what they were like. They tasted okay, but never became a favorite food item.

But on another Thanksgiving I decided to try something really crazy. I cooked some of those local sweet potatoes, soaking them overnight in yellow food coloring mixed with a little red. By next morning, the color seemed exactly right. I then candied them with brown sugar, cinnamon and butter. We had visitors from out of town for dinner, and I loved it when they enthusiastically asked how we had managed to find sweet potatoes in Pakistan.

Living in Murree during the summer gave me opportunity to make jam and jellies from the blackberries growing wild on the mountain side. Enterprising villagers had learned how much foreigners liked these berries. They picked them during the short season and came to our door, selling them. Cucumbers also were available and I made pickles every year. These items added variety to our menus.

These memories focus on Western foods. We also loved Pakistani food and there was a wide variety. And we tried to serve at least one home cooked Pakistani meal a week.

Invitations to visit a Pakistani home were always welcomed with enthusiasm. We knew we would get the very best food. I loved afternoon teas in the homes of my women friends. Typically, the menu would include *seekh kebobs*, *shami kebobs*, *samosas*, *pakoras*, and dried fruits and nuts. We also were served cups of steaming hot tea cooked with large quantities of milk and sugar.

I never learned to eat or enjoy some of the more exotic delicacies. Although it is eaten from time to time, fortunately I never had to confront a local Sindhi dish that featured sheep's eyes. An encounter with sheep's brains unnerved me enough.

For the most part, I thrived on Pakistani food and came to enjoy it immensely. The variety seemed endless, ranging from platters of rice cooked with a wide assortment of spices to every kind of curry, grilled meat, vegetables, and bread. Although Indian and Pakistani cuisine is now available in many parts of the United States, I enjoy cooking Pakistani food at home.

Cultural exchange is a two-way street and some of the best types of interaction among people have always involved food. Many years ago in Pakistan, I was asked to teach my women friends how to bake Western-style cookies, cake, and bread. In return, I insisted they give me lessons on how to prepare and cook their own food.

I have kept notes, collected recipes and bought cookbooks covering the entire range of South Asian cuisine. In retirement I continue to enjoy cooking and serving my friends and family this food. Perhaps more than anything, it is the sights, smells, and tastes I recreate in my kitchen that most remind me of the many years I spent in Pakistan.

Chapter Five

LANGUAGE

During the summer of 1955 we settled into a dormitory for women run by the United Church of Canada in Toronto for a six-week training course in linguistics. It was my first trip outside the United States. Right away there were unforeseen complications. Upon arrival we learned that I and our six-month old son David had been assigned to a room with another woman and two of her young children. Hu was assigned to another room with her husband and their young son. Both couples were astounded at the very thought of spending six weeks separated at a time when we desperately needed each other. The problem was that this residence was for women and women only. Men had never lived in the residence. There were no facilities for men.

The four of us sat down and discussed this awkward dilemma. We approached the supervisor who told us that arrangements could not be altered. Even a lecture on the sufferings and trials of missionary life did nothing to assuage us. Ultimately we came up with a plan that simply designated one bathroom at one end of the hall for men and at the other end one for the women. What a brilliant idea! It worked. And it took little time for us to switch our baggage from one room to another.

The weeks involved intense training in phonetics, language structure, and practice assimilation of actual languages (Vietnamese and Aymara, a South American Indian language). In addition, required reading, cultural anthropology, and other material relevant to the language learning problems we might face took almost all of our time.

For the first time in my life I had been exposed to a foreign language and the tonal Vietnamese presented a challenge for someone like me whose ability in musical sounds was somewhat limited. Nevertheless, I managed to complete the program with an average grade in language-learning ability.

The brief Toronto experience proved useful in preparing for the language challenges that lay ahead in Pakistan. As soon as we arrived in the hill station of Murree we were given a few days to settle in before embarking on learning a new language in earnest. We were to study Sindhi, one of Pakistan's several regional languages and spoken across the province of Sindh where we would live and work. An ancient language, it is steeped in culture and has a proud literary heritage as well as a poetic tradition rooted in some of the most prominent Sufi sages of the Indian subcontinent. Reading and writing from right to left in the Persian script demanded a complete re-orientation for our Western-oriented brains.

There was no school and almost no textual material in English for learning this language. Ancient language books left by colonial British scholars gave us a basis for study. An older New Zealand missionary, Dick Carson, had mastered the language and his offer of assistance was invaluable. Among our own peers was another brilliant linguist, Warren Webster. He prepared lessons a day or so ahead of us. Several young students from the province of Sindh had been hired to serve as informants. They had no teaching experience but were invaluable in drilling us in pronunciations and word usage. Unabashedly they laughed at our attempts to speak in their language. Getting to know and understand us was as important as our getting to know and understand them. Our questions, in the Sindhi language of course, helped us in our adjustments into their culture. In turn, they welcomed the opportunity to practice their English on us.

I'll never forget the experience of inviting them to dinner. Local food is hot with spices. Therefore, our food is nothing but bland and unappetizing for them. Barbecue was the only food I could think of that might appeal to them. Pulling out my best recipe for barbecue sauce, I attempted to prepare a meal with chicken and rice. Tossing some extra red pepper into the mix, I was confident. Sure enough, they thoroughly enjoyed the food--so much so that it was not at all embarrassing for them to spit the bones out the open window near the dining table. When finished eating, they drank a big glass of water and let out a resounding burp. That was the ultimate compliment. My cooking was a success.

I wish I could say that my language learning was as easy as preparation for that dinner. It was difficult from the beginning. Foreign languages were uncommon in the environment in which I grew up. I made every possible effort to grasp the language and I worked hard.

When the cool summer months in the mountains of Murree began to turn colder, it was time to go to the plains of Sindh. Once again, local students served as our informants and tutors as we settled into life in Ratodero. Every day, we learned new vocabulary words and tried to make sense of the complicated Sindhi grammar that in no way resembled English. Gradually, the essential words of day to day living became part of our conversations. Periodically we were given progress tests. I was slow and wondered if I would ever be able to communicate.

Learning Sindhi was never easy but I determined to reach a level of communication. I kept trying, regardless of the mistakes I made. It was a good thing I could laugh at myself because I made a few bloopers along the way.

I will always remember the time that my language teacher, a lovely young college student, invited me to her home for tea. She had prepared an assortment of delicacies, some familiar and others not. Biting into the patty that resembled a crab cake, I found it to be quite tasty.

"What is this?" I asked in Sindhi.

She gave me a word I had not heard before. I was a total blank so she tried other words. In the end she gave me the word for intellect. Immediately I knew what I was eating brains - yes, sheep brains, a very fine delicacy served on special occasions.

Tasty or not, it was difficult psychologically to finish. Later in my experiences I found out that Pakistanis don't mind letting their host know when they are served food they don't like. There is no embarrassment whatsoever.

Requirements for reaching fluency and ability to use the language loomed over me. The missionary women who had children and home responsibilities were given leniency in these requirements. We had to pass the first year test before home leave which came at the end of four years. The men and singles had tougher requirements. They were required to pass the second year testing. Since they didn't have children or a husband, supposedly the single women had more time for study.

Because it was taking me longer, my colleagues joked about Hu getting to go on home leave without me. I really didn't know what would happen should I fail to pass that one year exam. The pressure was on me to finish and I worked extra hard. Having had one child with us on arrival in Pakistan and giving birth to two more did not make language learning any easier. However, it did help in learning new vocabulary related to home and family and my local women friends assisted me in learning those words not in our language syllabus. The local vernacular was often far different from what I learned in my language course, giving me an early lesson in the fact that there is sometimes a clear difference between formal language learning and the ability to communicate with people who themselves could not read or write.

When I finally qualified for that big first year exam (it took me three and a half years), I entered the exam room to find Warren Webster and two of the local informants who had taken me through the studies. I was more nervous than I had ever been in my life. My knees, under the table, were shaking like jelly. Sensing my nervousness and trying to help me, Warren gently eased me into the questions and we moved along. Translating from English to Sindhi and Sindhi to English I felt quite proud of myself and I began to relax.

Another section of the exam involved sight reading. Handing me a child's reader, I was given a few minutes to look at the short passage. I found familiar words along with unknown ones. Struggling to make sense of it all, I wanted to move on so I looked up and said, "I guess I'm ready." I began to read and translate. The truth was obvious. I did not know what I was reading. A very long word loomed before me and I blurted out, *mavo nashpotty* and before I could take a breath, the informants burst into uncontrollable laughter. Even Warren lost his composure and also laughed.

Stinging with embarrassment, I felt my face turning red, on fire. My knees shook so violently I felt the table move. None of the three examiners could look me in the face. I had no idea what I had said or how it fit into the context of the rest of the sentence.

Several minutes passed and we regrouped, even as the men continued to resist the urge to laugh. I thought I was reading the Sindhi word for *pear fruit*. In fact, the phrase that I was unable to comprehend and had simply guessed at was an English word written in the Sindhi script: *municipality*.

English words, whether written in the Sindhi or Urdu script, are often hard to recognize, especially for those just learning the language. Nevertheless, other parts of the exam went well. I was given passing marks, allowing me to accompany Hu on our first home leave after all.

During the ensuing years I became more at home in the language. I was able to speak and understand the vernacular effectively. Although I often wished I could read and write better, I accepted every opportunity to converse with my local friends, many of whom were illiterate. There was no subject which we could not discuss. Because I was able to drop my inhibitions and fears of making mistakes in speaking to women in their language, I forged ahead, making life-long friendships with countless women. To this day I miss those warm, intimate exchanges.

There were other languages in Pakistan. Urdu is, the language understood throughout the country. Hu, having mastered Sindhi (he helped to write a language book for others to learn Sindhi), had no problem learning Urdu. He conducted his ministry in both Sindhi and Urdu. I never studied Urdu. However, because Urdu is the language most Christians use in worship I assimilated enough to participate in worship. Singing the old hymns and psalms was uplifting and over time I comprehended most of what I sang. On occasion, the singing was in yet another language, Punjabi. This language was actually the mother tongue of the majority of Christians who had originally come from the province of Punjab, to the north of Sindh.

Because of my love for interacting with people and the propensity I have for talking, I grabbed every opportunity to become a part of any conversation and dialogue. I like to believe that the language of my heart somehow compensated for my deficiencies in a language I never fully mastered. Learning another language was a lifetime commitment and I thoroughly enjoyed the challenges I faced in communicating with the women who called me their friend.

Chapter Six

FRIENDS

My first four years in Pakistan were spent in language study. This period was also a time of adjustment, becoming familiar with new customs, learning how to run a household and trying to find my place in the small rural town in which we lived.

We arrived with an eighteen-month-old toddler and I gave birth to two more children within the next three years. Sickness took a toll as all of us came down with malaria, amoeba, and other disorders of one kind or another. Often, I was frustrated because I did not believe I was getting to know the local women as I had hoped.

Now and then my husband was invited to the homes of some of the men he had met. Frequently, I was invited to come along as well. At first, I sat in the room with the men as they visited. It was awkward. We were aware that men and women did not integrate socially. I felt ill at ease. The women were elsewhere in the house, preparing tea and snacks which were served to us, yet never showing their faces.

Later, when I became more at home conversing in the Sindhi language, I made a new effort to meet the women. Whenever Hu received invitations including me, he suggested that I would be happy to come if I could meet the women in the household. This worked very well and I began to enjoy such visits. At last, I had found opportunity to make friendships and explore the lives of those around me.

I began to invite women into my home. They were fascinated with everything in the house. I had to show them our kerosene stove and refrigerator as well as other kitchen gadgets. There was also great interest in our bedrooms.

Most of these women had never met a foreigner. They had many questions, some of them personal. For example, no one was embarrassed to ask how much money my husband earned. Similarly, if I served something they did not like, they would tell me so without hesitation. My freckles intrigued them as they had never seen freckles before. Actually, when they saw my freckles, they initially thought I had some disease.

There were more than a few misconceptions about the West. Now, with a westerner living among them, there was an interest in verifying all they had been told about us. One common rumor was that the milk powder American foreign assistance programs were distributing across Pakistan came from pigs.

"Do you drink pig's milk?" I was once asked.

"No," I replied.

"Then who drinks pig's milk?"

"Baby pigs," I answered, without hesitation. "Baby pigs drink pig's milk."

Since there is no distinction in Pakistan between Islam and the State, most of our early contacts assumed we spoke on behalf of our government. In fact, it was often initially assumed that we not only had been sent to Pakistan by the U.S. government but were paid by the U.S. government as well. Although I felt these questions were sometimes silly, I had to remember that in 1956 I did not know very much about Pakistan and the local women did not know much about America.

———

I tried to share as much as I could with my emerging circle of friends, partly because there were a million questions that I also wanted to ask. After all, I reasoned, turnabout is fair play. Some women expressed fear that we ate pork in our house, something strictly forbidden in Islam. My assurances that we did not serve pork in our house relieved them, but I'm not sure they entirely believed it. I served home-baked cakes and cookies when women visited. I had to learn how to cook in Pakistan. We were practically newlyweds when we arrived and most of the cooking I had done in the United States came from packaged mixes.

Both my mother and my mother-in-law were excellent cooks and had taken charge of the kitchen on Christmas and other special holidays. Baking cookies and cakes from scratch on a kerosene stove presented challenges. In particular, it seemed nearly impossible to get the right temperature. Sometimes the stove got too hot, filling the kitchen with black smoke and ruining whatever I was cooking at the time. Like other middle and upper class families, we had a cook who helped in the kitchen. Entertaining was much easier with a cook. He was invaluable as he could also prepare local delicacies.

Conversations at these tea parties centered on children, home, cooking, sewing, and all the everyday concerns women are involved in when living in a small and defined community. I was enjoying life in our small provincial town set in a remote part of rural Pakistan.

Our initial four years in Pakistan were followed by a year of furlough in the United States. After twelve busy months of visiting family, churches, and refresher courses relevant to missions, we returned to Sindh in 1961, this time moving to Shikarpur, a larger town that offered new experiences. I felt much better prepared. I had learned more about the customs and traditions of women living in a Muslim society. I had also made progress in the Sindhi language. My three children were older. I was eager and quite ready to embark upon establishing friendships with the women in my new town. Still, I had arrived in Shikarpur without knowing a soul. It was difficult to know where to begin. However, word must have circulated about the foreigners who had just moved to town.

One important event happened late in October. Our colleagues Ralph and Polly Brown had come with their children for a visit. We had chosen to live and work in Pakistan and we wanted our children to adjust and adapt to their new surroundings. At the same time, we also celebrated American customs, traditions, and holidays. On this particular day, I had prepared a little Halloween party, complete with simple costumes and games. The children dressed up in make-do costumes such as witches, goblins, and black cats and were having a great time. Suddenly, the courtyard bell rang and a note was passed through the door.

"My sister is visiting me from Karachi and we are bored stiff," read the note, written in English. "I heard that you are new in our town and that you are English. May we come to your home?"

I was amazed. At the same time I was a little disappointed that the children's party was being interrupted. I had been anxious to meet women and with this note came the chance that I had been waiting for. And, this might be an opportunity that would not be repeated any time soon.

"Please do come and bring your sister with you," I replied in a note of my own. "I will be most happy to meet you."

Quickly I ended the party and tried to get things in order.

Improbably, this single event marked the beginning of a wide network of friendships with Muslim women living in Shikarpur. Their generosity by including me in their special events provided a window into a world that I otherwise would never have experienced. Indeed, the young woman called Mona (not her real name) who sent me the note became the closest friend I ever had in Pakistan. She also became a willing and trusted source of information for the many questions I had about the customs and traditions of our corner in Upper Sindh. Through her, I met other women who enriched my life immeasurably.

Because of these friendships, I found as much acceptance in Pakistan as any foreign woman could hope to have. An indication of acceptance occurred when at one of my tea parties one of the women asked me, "Bettie, may I have a clean sheet?" Of course I was surprised but only momentarily. The *Azan* had sounded from a nearby mosque. It was time for the late afternoon call to prayer.

Quickly, I ran to the linen closet, chose a fresh white sheet and handed it to Sofia. She took it, clutched her *duputta* over her head and went into the bedroom and from there to the bathroom where she performed ablutions; washing her hands, face, ears and feet. Then, she spread the sheet out on the bedroom floor. Kneeling on the sheet, she faced *Mecca* and said her prayers. When she was finished, she joined the party group. Others did not heed the call to prayer. Sofia was religious and she never missed a call to prayer at other times in my home.

My new-found friend, Mona, had grown up in some of the larger cities of Pakistan. Her father had been in the police force and served as chief in various assignments. She came from a large family and had several brothers and sisters. Her sisters had married well and continued to live in urban areas. As for herself, she had been married to an older man who was widowed with two small children. She told me that, although she agreed to the proposal, she felt apprehensive and afraid of marrying an older man with children.

Mona's husband was from a large family of landlords. They were prominent and well known in legal and educational circles. However, her own husband had remained in the village ancestral home and received only a minimal education. He owned a small business that involved running a bus service over the dusty and poorly maintained rural roads in the province. The modest earnings from this business, supplemented with periodic remunerations from the family land holdings, provided the family with income.

Early in our friendship, she shared events from her life with me. One of the more revealing ones was her wedding night. At the time, it was traditional to inspect for blood on the sheets on which the couple spent their first night to confirm that the young bride was in fact a virgin. She said her mother-in-law had indeed checked, just to make sure. She had not seen her husband before the wedding and, of course, she was afraid. Thankfully, her husband from the beginning was kind and thoughtful, never aggressive.

Becoming a mother to the two young children from his previous marriage was a challenge. By the time we met, she had children of her own. During the years we lived in Shikarpur, she had a total of five biological children: two girls and three boys. Some were the same age as my children and they often played together. She was a good mother and a loving wife. I was surprised and pleased to meet a couple who seemed very much in love. Theirs was a positive testimony for an arranged marriage. They were devoted to each other, and the happy family they raised and nurtured reflected this love and devotion.

I was often invited to the home of my new friend, and through her, met other women and was invited into their homes as well. Wedding celebrations in particular were a special time. As the number of invitations increased, I realized I needed to expand my wardrobe and I was excited about getting it all together. Shikarpur may have seemed to outsiders like a provincial backwater town, but the women were very fashion conscious and dressed in the latest styles under the long black veil known as a *burka* which they wore when leaving their house.

I subscribed to a slick English women's magazine published in Karachi to help keep me in the loop. On occasion, I even designed my own outfits. I felt honored to be part of the community. Often, I entertained with tea parties of my own. Of course, I had to reassure my new friends that, when they entered my courtyard and home, there would be no men around.

Our home was set up in the same style as the locals. First of all, we had a room just inside our walled courtyard designated as my husband's reception room. Called the *otak*, it was nicely furnished with a sofa, chairs, lamps, tables, pictures on the wall, and a locally made carpet. Whenever a male came from the outside to the courtyard door, he was directed immediately to this room.

Local men very rarely came inside our home, and then only if no local women were visiting. Whenever a woman came to the door, she came directly into our home. Even Hu was not in the house when there were women visitors. Instead, he worked in the *otak*. During all the years we lived in Shikarpur, he met no more than half a dozen local Muslim women. In each case, the women were related to men he had formed a friendship with, to such an extent they were willing to introduce him to their wife.

Trusted servants were sometimes exempt from the general prohibition on any male ever laying eyes on a woman. Even so, there were boundaries never crossed. Eye contact was never made. Touching was unacceptable. Our household helper served as a cook and also shopped in the bazaar daily for fresh fruits, vegetables and meat. Another male helper served outside as a gardener and watchman. He was also assigned the task of opening the door to the courtyard whenever the brass bell was pulled, announcing the arrival of a visitor.

It was acceptable for me to have these two male servants around because my women friends also had male servants in their household. Indeed, every middle-class home employed servants. Usually, female servants took care of children, washed clothes, cleaned, and cooked. Men served as watchmen, drivers, and gardeners and sometimes as cook. Servants were indispensable and became very much like a member of the family. They were trusted and taken care of in sickness and in health.

Our servants became acquainted with the servants of my friends and helped maintain the relationship. We had no telephone during those years and the only way to communicate was by hand-delivered notes. Our watchman became a special delivery mail carrier, riding a bicycle all over town to deliver notes of one kind or another. Although we had a Land Rover, it was mostly used for out-of-town trips. My husband also chose to go about town on his bicycle, becoming a well-known sight as we slowly became part of the Shikarpur community.

It was not acceptable for a woman to ride about town on a bicycle or travel alone. Instead, Baroo, our outside servant, called for a horse-drawn *tonga* whenever I needed one. He also accompanied me, sitting up front with the *tonga* driver. Sometimes he would sit with other servants while I visited. On other occasions, he would leave as soon as I entered the courtyard, returning later at a pre-determined time. This ritual was repeated countless times during the many years we lived in Shikarpur.

While adopting many local customs, I never wore a *burka*. In retrospect, at times wearing one might have been useful—by hiding behind the veil, I could at least have avoided the stares from men and boys as well as the attention of children playing in the streets. However, I always wore local clothing, the traditional *shalwar, kameez* along with a *duputta* wrapped around my head and upper body. I also wore big sun glasses that covered my eyes. Baroo often kept onlookers from getting too close to me. The *tonga* swiftly moved through the streets. I was safe as I went about town in this carriage.

The women arriving at the courtyard door were always veiled in a *burka*, covering them from head to foot. Walking across the courtyard, they removed the *burka* immediately on reaching the verandah. We then settled down to an afternoon of fun, friendship, and tea. I loved every minute of these visits and will always be indebted to Mona for her love and friendship, and for opening up this world of women for me.

Mona was a woman of character and she built character into her children. She accepted her stepchildren as her own. We spent hours talking, discussing everything from family life to religious beliefs. She

77

admired our modest home and always commented on the way I had decorated it, using indigenous furnishings, accessories, and fabrics. As her family grew, she moved into a larger house. She asked me to help with the interior decorating. It was fun decorating a room for the boys, using local and inexpensive fabrics. The little girls were thrilled with the ruffles and feminine pastel printed materials we chose.

When we got to the master bedroom, I suggested moving the bed from one wall to another, giving prominence to the beautifully carved bed.

"We can't do that," she quickly said, placing her hand over her mouth in shock and consternation, much like our heaven forbid.

"Why not?" I asked.

The problem, as she pointed out, was that placing the bed against that particular wall meant that those sleeping in it would have their feet pointing toward *Mecca*. This is forbidden in Islam. Of course, the bed stayed where it was. Later I learned the same principle holds true when arranging a bathroom. The toilet must be fixed so that it does not face *Mecca*.

Our enduring friendship involved the kitchen as well. We had imported a kerosene stove, looking very much like a gas range. It was yellow and white and had four burners as well as an oven. It was such an improvement over the first portable two-burner stove and portable oven we had used for four years. Neither bottled gas nor natural gas had been delivered to our area, though it had recently been discovered at Sui in Baluchistan not many miles away. Most homes in small town Pakistan during the 1960s, even middle-class homes, cooked over an open fire using dried cow dung as well as precious wood for fuel. Even so, feasts were cooked over an open fire. There were no ovens in the kitchens.

My favorite dessert of all time is baked custard prepared over an open fire. Two large heavy aluminum pots were used to form something like a double boiler. With water in the bottom vessel, the custard was in the top vessel with a cover. Coals of fire were placed on the cover. The fire below was kept at a steady temperature, ensuring perfect custard. As I write this, I drool just thinking about it.

One day Mona asked if I would bake a batch of cookies for her. She promised to bring all the ingredients and help me. It was a simple request and we soon found ourselves in the kitchen stirring up a batch of snicker doodles, the easiest recipe I could find. It wasn't long before requests came from other friends. They also wanted to learn how to make cookies.

At times, my kitchen looked almost like a factory production. Up to half a dozen women arrived on a pre-arranged day, laden with ingredients based on a recipe I had provided beforehand. I tied an apron on each one of them and we got to work. As always, working in the kitchen involved conversation. We covered every possible topic, including serious matters such as religion and problems facing the country to the latest Shikarpur gossip. At the end of each session, each woman left with a batch of homemade cookies for their family to enjoy.

Soon we went from cookies to cake. Oven temperatures are important for cakes. My kerosene stove was not always reliable. Nevertheless, we tried out several recipes and met with some success. Later, we progressed to quick breads and cinnamon rolls. In time, bottled gas was introduced to Shikarpur and our informal cooking circle was almost certainly the first to use it, buying stoves and ovens to enhance their cooking. Traditionally, one thinks of a teacher's success by success of the students. If that is the criteria, I achieved notable success because, over time, these women became true experts.

Even as I introduced certain Western foods, my friends showed me the best of Pakistani cooking. Always, the most delicious of foods were sent to us on the various Muslim holidays. We were overwhelmed with their generosity. I knew almost certainly that it was the women in the household, not a servant, who had prepared the food because, on such occasions, they wanted to serve only the very best.

Following their custom of sharing special foods on a holiday, I also prepared platters of cookies of my own for Christmas and Easter. Along with baked goods, I sometimes enclosed an annual calendar published by a Christian publishing house in Lahore. The design incorporated typical Pakistani themes, for example, birds of Pakistan for one year and flowers of Pakistan for another. This gesture was well received and allowed me to explain something of our traditions and beliefs to my friends and neighbors, even as I was becoming more familiar with theirs.

Christmas was always a special time for us, comparable to the big *Eid* celebrations which our Muslim neighbors observed following the month of *Ramadan*. I invited my women friends and their children to celebrate Christmas with me at some point during the holiday season. Our home was decked out for the occasion, using a combination of imported ornaments as well as suitable local ones. Food was important and always a selection of cookies cut in the shape of stars, trees, and gingerbread people. Instead of the usual cups of hot tea, I pulled out my punch bowl and served red punch. Surprisingly, my attempt at party games caught on. For some reason, guessing how many pieces of candy in a jar proved to be very popular. Everyone hoped their guess would be closest so that they could take the jar of candy home with them.

Over time, Mona became the special friend everyone hopes to find a least once in their life. We trusted each other and she shared her struggles with me. One concern was her stepson who had become addicted to drugs. He was a young man who somehow failed to fit into the society around him. He turned to drugs. Every kind of drug was easily available. Eventually he died while in a stupor. Heartbroken with grief, she told me how she and her husband had tried desperately to get help for him.

A few years later, Mona's husband died of a heart attack and she was left, a young widow with six growing children. As the children grew, so did the need for their education. The school situation in Shikarpur was not good and ultimately, after lengthy deliberations, she decided to move to Karachi where there were many more opportunities.

Increased opportunities also brought greater financial worries. It was possible to live well on a limited income in a small provincial town. However, living in an international mega city like Karachi presented an entirely different set of challenges. Income from her husband's joint family enterprises had dwindled. In addition, unresolved inheritance issues lingered and created additional problems. Life was a struggle. Nevertheless, Mona managed to get a teacher's certificate and found a low-paying job in a primary school. Somehow, she managed to provide for her children and gave them a good basic education.

As with any parent in Pakistan, she was concerned about getting her girls married to suitable partners. The oldest of the children, the step-daughter, was the first to get married and she married a decent, hard-working young man. Mona's own two daughters were attractive and intelligent. She could easily have found suitable matches for them, but she did not want them to marry at a young age. They could have done well in college. That was not possible for them. Mona encouraged them to seek employment, something unheard of in her circle of family and friends. Both eventually became airline stewardesses, an honorable occupation but one frowned upon in many middle and upper class communities. The fact that they traveled as single young women throughout Pakistan and into neighboring countries also brought criticism. The consensus was that well-bred girls from good families did not engage in such employment. Nursing was also frowned upon. These occupations required serving men from all walks of life and were unacceptable. Nonetheless, Mona held her head high and the girls thrived in their work. Their income provided much needed income for the family and their living standard greatly improved.

Mona saved money for the girls and eventually bought an apartment in their names. She guided her sons into marketable skills. The oldest migrated to the United States for college, got his green card and later became an American citizen. When it was time for him to marry, his mother arranged for a beautiful girl from Pakistan as his bride.

The other two boys joined their older brother in his business ventures in America. They too married Pakistani girls, arranged by their mother. Eventually, she also arranged marriages for her daughters.

We attended the wedding of Mona's oldest daughter in Karachi. Interestingly, her husband came from outside the family's own language and cultural community. Her husband was an only son with a widowed mother and an older married sister who worked for a foreign airline. The transition to a home where both the mother-in-law and the sister-in-law lived was difficult. An incident occurred at the wedding and gave me a clue for future conflicts. The handsome groom wanted to take his gorgeous bride for a ride in the flower-decorated car. He helped her into the car and sat down beside her under the wheel. The older sister came out of the house and promptly vetoed the idea. They were not allowed to go alone. Someone had to sit in the car with them. Resistance to elements of cultural changes had begun. The couple eventually moved into their own apartment and began an independent life.

Their marriage has been happy, blessed with bright intelligent children and employment for both of them. Obviously they love each other deeply. They have enjoyed travel, including opportunities to spend time in the United States. Their children attend colleges in the United States and have excelled academically.

Soon after their wedding, Abdul the young groom, asked me to give him some advice since he had observed our happy marriage. I thought of some words of wisdom my husband had received: "The best thing you can do for your children is to love their mother." Throughout the ensuing years Abdul told me over and over he had tried to follow that advice.

As Mona watched her children enter into their chosen occupations and her grandchildren grow up, she continued to confide in me some of the struggles both she and the children faced: emigrating, green cards, family responsibilities. She always asked me to pray for her. Her mission was to see all of the children well-married and settled into adult life. She looked forward to grandchildren. Finally she settled with her oldest son and his family in America. The other children have also emigrated with the exception of one who remains in Pakistan, looking after family interests there.

In more recent years, Mona and I often talked by phone. She even came to visit me in Macon, Georgia. She has been as interested in my children and their welfare as I have been in hers. Her children call me "auntie" and Hu is called "uncle."

During one visit to Pakistan, Mona became ill and needed surgery. She was diagnosed with cancer, suffered through chemotherapy and realized that she faced a losing battle. She returned to the United States for her final months.

Her last words to me are especially poignant and move me to tears everytime I remember them: "Bettie, I am not afraid to die. God has answered our prayers. Thank God, all my children have married good and decent people. I have been blessed in my life. Thank God, I had a good husband and good children. Thank you for being my friend."

With Mona's death, I lost a special friend. Her children keep in touch and visit sometimes. They beg us to come and visit them. The grandchildren are now reaching marriageable age. Mona would be very proud of her family and their accomplishments. Birth, marriage, life, death: the cycle continues and Mona's legacy lives on.

———

One of the women in my circle of close friends in Shikarpur was not a local. Her family had come to Pakistan during the great migration accompanying independence in 1947, when Muslim majority areas of British India had been carved out to form an Islamic state. Many Muslims living in other parts of India moved to Pakistan at independence, becoming *muhajirs* or refugees. A large number of them settled in our town, making new lives for themselves in Pakistan, taking the place of the Hindus who had migrated to India at partition. Even more than fifty years later, the children of the refugees who arrived at independence are still called *muhajirs*.

The *muhajir* woman I met—let me call her Hina—exemplified the culture her parents and grandparents strove to maintain. She spoke a refined and classical Urdu as well as Punjabi rather than the Sindhi language of our area. The differences were also apparent in her dress, habits, and food. The habit of chewing *paan* was common for them but not for Sindhis. *Betel nut* is crushed, mixed with slate lime or lemon juice and served on a *paan* leaf. The *betel nut* produced a red color and red betel juice could often be seen dripping from the mouths of those who used it.

I tried to chew *betel nut* once. It caused my mouth to pucker as if I had eaten a green persimmon. I found it disgusting. However, as I thought about it, I remembered that my grandmother used to dip snuff. It sometimes dripped, but she always had a handkerchief in her pocket to keep her mouth wiped. My grandmother loved to hug us and when she came to visit we would often run and hide because we did not want to be around the snuff. With that perspective, I was able to tolerate the habit of chewing *paan* and *betel nut*, although I still considered it unsanitary and probably a bit harmful.

Hina was very hospitable to me, perhaps recognizing that I too was a stranger and a newcomer to Shikarpur. I also heard endless stories from her about the India they had left behind and of the problems they faced in Pakistan, their newly adopted country.

One issue was that of property. Theoretically, the *muhajirs* were to be given properties of equal value to those left behind in India. In fact, Hina and her husband lived with his parents, in a nice, large house within the city. They owned farmland also and were clearly financially secure.

Hina's husband was in a serious farming accident and almost died. He had been run over by a tractor. Devastated, Hina asked me to pray for his recovery. We all prayed for him and after a lengthy recuperation he recovered.

Following her husband's recovery, Hina planned a special thanksgiving service to which she invited all her friends. It was called a *majilis*. I went and a host of other women also came; some I knew and others were strangers. This was a new experience for me. The atmosphere on arrival was much more subdued than that of the usual tea party. Carpets were laid out and we sat on the floor with our legs crossed. A woman dressed in white, her head completely covered and wearing no shoes, sat on a raised dais. She held an open *Quran* in her lap. When all the guests had arrived, she began to read from the *Quran*. Gradually the recitation became a chant. I did not understand the Arabic words, but knew from the mood and reverence that this was a very solemn religious praise service. Following a benediction, the service was over; we greeted each other and were served a lavish tea.

As Hina and I became close friends we enjoyed each other's company over a number of years. She had a young son and doted on him. Everything he could possibly want she gave to him. He was sent away to a boarding school at an early age. Education was an important value for the family.

She herself was physically large, dressed extravagantly and wore an enormous array of fine jewelry, all of it gold, and much of it studded with precious and semi-precious stones.

Once when we were leaving for the United States, she gave me a long list of items, requesting that I look for them in America. The list included toys for her children. However, there was one item underscored twice, indicating it should receive the highest priority. The important item was a girdle–she wanted to tuck her large and buxom body into a tight fitting girdle.

Hina loved her husband. Yet, there was an aura of sadness and restlessness about her. In time, she confided to me doubts of her husband's love. She said he was cold towards her and did not talk to her very much. She also worried about the possibility of him taking another wife. After all, he was prosperous and it was not at all unusual for a man of his status and means to have more than one wife. Islam allows a man to have up to four wives.

One day the extent of Hina's worries came to a climax. I received a note asking me to come immediately to her home. She was in bed, crying and groggy. She had attempted to take her life by over-dosing on sleeping pills. The family was distraught as well as fearful the neighbors would learn of the episode. As best as I could, I tried to console my friend. She came through the crisis and once again devoted her attention to her family.

After I left Shikarpur, I lost contact with Hina. Still, I have often thought about her over the years. I wonder how her children turned out and whether they still consider themselves as refugees in Pakistan. In retrospect, I can see that her life mirrored that of others who had arrived in Pakistan to make a new life and yet faced disappointments along the way.

———

We also enjoyed friendships within the Pakistani Christian community. Some fifteen or so miles to the west of Shikarpur, toward Jacobabad and the border with the province of Baluchistan, was a very small town on the edge of the desert called Sultankot. An elderly Christian woman with grey hair worked there. Known to everyone in the community as either "Auntie Grace" or simply "Auntie," she had already lived in Sultankot for many years before we arrived. Along with her were two educated nephews named Basil and Leonard as well as two grandsons, sons of her son who lived in Karachi. Apparently, the parents of the nephews had died years before. We never learned anything about them.

The fact that she provided a home for her relatives was not unusual. Employment is often hard to find in Pakistan and families will split up if work is available elsewhere. The two nephews, by now grown up, were still single. They found jobs as private tutors for the well-to-do Muslim families living in the area. Christian teachers were appreciated and highly regarded. The two grandsons were also tutored by their uncles. Everyone seemed to have ajusted well and the family lived together happily in this environment.

Hanging over the door of Auntie's house was a sign: Red Cross Maternity Home. On entering the courtyard of the large mud structure, there was a clear division. One side was set up as a ward with hospital beds and the other side served as living quarters for the family. Auntie Grace was a nurse-midwife. For a generation, she had delivered just about every child, not only in Sultankot but also in surrounding villages. Patients often arrived by *tonga* or ox-cart to have Auntie deliver their babies. Unless there were problems, most women stayed only a few hours and then returned home. There was not a hint of modern equipment to be seen anywhere. Simple medications were on hand and a frail woman was around to assist.

When American missionaries first arrived in Shikarpur in the mid 1950's, they were informed about the Christian family living in Sultankot. At their request, we began to go there each Sunday for a worship service with them. During the winter months, Auntie served up steaming cups of hot tea. During the hot summer months, she provided a local soft drink made of rose water. I loved the hot tea but could barely tolerate the rose water. Besides, I was not sure of the source of the ice. Most probably it did not come from boiled water. Over time, I found it increasingly difficult to pretend I liked the drink. Reflecting that my Pakistani friends seemed to have no problem expressing their own likes and dislikes, I eventually found the nerve to tell Auntie that I could no longer drink the rose water.

Auntie came from the Anglican Church tradition. We were Baptists and from a very different background. Yet, we were all Christians and sometimes incorporated parts of the *Book of Common Prayer* into our service. Always, we began with Urdu hymns. The early nineteenth century missionaries to the Indian subcontinent had translated many English hymns into both Urdu and Punjabi. We could easily follow the tunes. One of the hymns had been set to the tune of "Oh my Darling Clementine." Our children could hardly contain themselves, stifling their laughter whenever this song was included on the list of hymns for the day.

Singing is often the highlight of any worship service in Pakistan, and not only because unlikely tunes sometimes pop up in unlikely places. Over time, an indigenous tradition of singing had emerged, especially in the Punjab where it was possible to find entire villages that were largely Christian. Perhaps the early Scottish missionaries also had a part in spreading their love of the Psalms, translating them into both Urdu and Punjabi and then setting them to music. We easily learned to love the truly wonderful music contained in what is known as the *Punjabi Psalter*.

Despite the small congregation and overwhelming sense of isolation, we enjoyed the hundreds of services that we attended with Auntie in Sultankot over the years. Following a time of singing, we recited the Lord's Prayer together in Urdu. Hu then spoke for about twenty minutes. The brief worship concluded with another hymn and prayer.

Occasionally, a woman came into the maternity home during the service. If that happened, Auntie quickly left for her duties. Sometime we arrived to find her attending a patient and we would wait for her to finish her work before beginning the service. She never complained. Her remuneration was limited. The government did provide housing while the added income from the nephews' tutoring gave them something approaching a middle-class existence. However, it was Auntie's loyalty, commitment and long hours that left a lasting impression on all of us. An unsung hero, her work and commitment were never recognized by anyone–except for the thousands of anonymous women living in and around Sultankot for whom she was never anything less than a devoted saint.

We became like family with Auntie and her family. Our children enjoyed going there each Sunday and when relatives visited from Karachi at Christmas we celebrated together. Relatives from the big city brought fruit cake, special cookies and other treats. On one trip some important items were left on the train and the whole family became terribly upset. In an effort to calm the distraught family, Hu suggested we pray together. We also went to the train station and alerted railway authorities of the loss. Our quick action paid off. The items were retrieved at the next station, given to the conductor on the first train returning to Sultankot and all was well. We have never forgotten this incident.

Auntie's older nephew had never married nor did he show any interest in getting married. However, she wanted her younger nephew, Basil, to marry. She asked our help in finding a suitable bride. Old age was creeping up on her and the nephews needed a woman to help them in the years ahead.

We began to enquire and in time were able to convey this need to others who could follow through on the cultural aspects of arranging a marriage. We were delighted with the young woman who was chosen. Catherine had been an orphan adopted by a Christian couple in Karachi, given a loving home life and educated in mission schools. Now she was a teacher. Auntie approved the match and preparations began for the celebration of the marriage, held in the Anglican Cathedral in Karachi. Following the festivities, the couple returned to Sultankot and took up residence with Auntie in the living quarters of the maternity home.

Sultankot was a difficult place for Catherine to live as she had been brought up in the city where she enjoyed relative freedom. Auntie was sensitive to the situation, understanding the need for the young married couple to live separately. She encouraged them to move to Shikarpur and they did. We saw more of them and they became helpful in the local congregation. They appeared to be adjusting well. Auntie wanted to hear news of an impending pregnancy, but it never came.

One Sunday, on our way to Sultankot for the regular worship service, Catherine gasped out loud. Turning around to see what was happening, I saw that she was covering her eyes with her hands.

"What is wrong?" I asked.

"Mrs. Addleton, I saw an owl," she replied with a troubled expression verging on horror and alarm. "An owl in daylight is a very bad omen. It means there will be a death." Despite my best efforts, I could not reassure her.

We continued on to Sultankot and to Auntie's place, conducted the worship service and returned home. I never thought of it again. However, Catherine was obviously brooding about seeing an owl during the broad daylight hours.

Basil, the young husband, was dealing with his own psychological issues. At times, it appeared that he was suffering from depression. He told us his father and other men in the family had died young, about the same age as he was now reaching. He was obsessed with the thought of dying young.

Early one afternoon we received a message from Catherine, asking us to come quickly and bring a doctor. Immediately we informed our missionary doctor and we went to Basil's home, only to find him dead. He had died of a heart attack. Catherine was inconsolable.

"I knew it. I knew it," she cried. "The owl; I saw an owl," she moaned.

Immediately, we informed Auntie who in turn stoically informed her other relatives. Missionary colleagues built a wooden coffin and lined it with cloth. There was no funeral home; close friends and relatives cared for the dead. My husband helped bathe the body and prepare it for burial.

As custom dictates, the body would have to be buried within twenty-four hours. The funeral would take place in Sukkur, a larger town on the Indus River to the east and about twenty four miles away. Sukkur, the largest city in Upper Sindh, had a large Anglican church and a well established Christian community numbering in the hundreds and perhaps thousands.

The night before the funeral, we gathered at Auntie's home in Sultankot. It seemed the entire village came to mourn with us. I hardly slept that night. Catherine wailed, throwing herself at Auntie's feet, begging her to allow her to be her servant.

All of us knew very well that in this culture a widow—whether Muslim, Christian or Hindu—faced heartaches and insurmountable problems. A young and attractive widow such as Catherine was especially vulnerable. There would be no place for her in Auntie's village. Had she been Hindu, the thought of throwing herself on her husband's funeral pyre might have crossed her mind. Had she been Muslim, the possibility of marrying her husband's brother might have been considered. Being Christian did not relieve her of anxiety. Where would she go next? What was to become of her? These concerns weighed heavily on Catherine's mind and heart and they were our concerns also.

Next morning, we all drove to the Anglican Church in Sukkur for the funeral. The local priest conducted the service. As we huddled around the grave site for the final prayer, someone noticed that the hole dug for the coffin was too small. We waited as a larger hole was dug. Friends and family gathered for the final act of lowering the coffin into the grave. When it was set in its place, each of us picked up a clod of dirt and dropped it into the grave–ashes to ashes, dust to dust. Fresh flowers were placed on top of the fresh mound of earth.

We all had feelings of emptiness and sadness as we turned from the grave and walked back to our vehicles for the drive home. Auntie and her family came with us to Shikarpur, where we had prepared lunch for everyone. Later, Hu and other colleagues drove them back to Sultankot. Catherine also went with them. She had no other place to go.

We helped Catherine as she moved her belongings from their house in Shikarpur to Auntie's house. Everyone wanted to know if Catherine was pregnant. Had she been pregnant, a child would have offered some consolation. However, it was not to be. As a matter of fact, Catherine had told us her husband was afraid to have sexual relations, afraid that he might have a heart attack. Judging from conversations with her, it is doubtful the marriage was ever consummated, an issue that might have been a deciding factor in some of the decisions Catherine made later, when she found herself a young and attractive Christian widow alone.

Catherine first stayed with Auntie a short while and then moved in with us for a week or so before joining a Christian family in another town. Eventually, she returned to Hyderabad where she had been teaching before her marriage. We corresponded for a while. We were heartbroken to learn she had married a Muslim and had gotten herself into a very unhappy situation. Often, we asked others about her and wished we could see her again. It never happened.

Auntie outlived both Basil and Leonard. She was a widow but she never told us anything about her husband. A person of selfless sacrifice and dedication, she faced tragedy in her own life yet somehow managed to overcome it.

When we finally left Shikarpur, Auntie prepared a special tea for us in Sultankot as a farewell. After tea she handed us a basket in which huddled a chicken with its legs tied together. There were tears in our eyes as we hugged and said our final good byes.

Just as we were getting into our Land Rover, Auntie reached out and forced something into my hands. "This is for Nancy," she said.

It was a wad of crumpled newspaper. I thanked her, realizing something was inside the paper.

Down the road and out of sight, I opened the paper. A beautiful gold filigree ring studded with tiny precious rubies lay in the old newspaper. It was an old ring, very likely one that Auntie had received on her wedding day many decades ago. She was gifting it to our daughter. Nancy still has the ring, a token and a memory of the love surrounding this gift to her from Auntie many years ago.

—

I never learned the proper name of an elderly Sindhi woman whom I always called *Mai*. *Mai* is a term of respect and endearment used entirely for women. Jesus used this word when, dying on the cross, he called out to his mother. The English translations usually have him saying "woman." To me, the Sindhi term is a touching term, capturing the feeling of respect that Jesus had for his mother. A lot of Sindhi women were called *Mai*, woman.

She, in turn, called me *Beyti*, meaning daughter and pronounced almost exactly like my own name, Bettie.

I first saw her when she came to my home as a servant accompanying one of my women friends. Although she came with her mistress, she was never a part of the social gathering. Servants always stayed in the background, never missing the gossip going on among the middle and upper class women they served.

I have no idea why *Mai* decided to visit me on her own. Perhaps she found my attempts at speaking Sindhi novel. Certainly, the dialect of Sindhi she spoke was very different from anything I had learned in the text books.

I invited her in and we sat down in comfortable chairs on the verandah. Rather, I sat down. I offered her a chair, but she chose to sit, legs crossed, on the floor. Always, it seemed, a servant had to sit lower than his or her master. We chatted and I offered her a cup of tea, which she refused.

Along the way, I had learned that offering a cup of tea to a visitor, whether known or unknown, is an important gesture of hospitality.

According to one of my local friends, to offer nothing reflects a very cold reception; to offer a glass of water is taken as a small measure of hospitality; and to offer a cup of hot tea indicates a high measure of cordiality and friendliness.

On this, a very hot day, *Mai* did not accept my offer of hot tea but did accept a glass of water. We first talked in a basic and introductory way, becoming more acquainted with each other, asking simple questions about children and family. She eyed me curiously and I wondered why she was visiting. She did not stay long, ending the conversation abruptly with the words, "I'm going now."

As she departed, I said I would welcome the opportunity to meet her again. She did, in fact, return on a number of occasions. A servant never has many free hours and, when *Mai* came to my house, I knew she was stealing scarce time from her mistress to visit me and might even face trouble because of it.

She arrived each time wearing a dusty and tattered white *burka*, the one that looks like a shuttle cock and has a tight-fitting cap, usually with embroidery, and small crocheted patches for the eyes. Her *shalwar, khameez,* and *duputta* were old, even ragged and never freshly laundered. I couldn't help but notice her feet. They were calloused; the skin was wrinkled and she wore open sandals. Throughout her life, she had worked hard and faced many hardships.

Mai reflected the life of many women in Pakistan—rural, illiterate, superstitious, poor, and hard-working. Through the years, I met other women just like her from both the Muslim and Christian community. Seemingly they have no voice and no one to speak for them. While a majority of my relationships were with middle and upper class women, I was also privileged to have known *Mai* and benefited from the knowledge she passed on to me.

Illiteracy is not a measure of intelligence. *Mai* was simple and illiterate, yet intelligent. She had a sharp mind. During evenings, when chores were finished, women like her, with light from a kerosene lantern, embroidered clothes for themselves and caps for the men. Sindh was famous for its mirror and embroidery work, all of it stitched by the women. It was also well-known for its appliquéd quilts made in many colors. Earning very little for their hours of work, handicrafts made by poor women found their way into specialty shops where wealthy Pakistanis as well as foreign tourists bought them.

Mai talked to me about areas of culture and tradition the more educated women hesitated to discuss. I had heard that men sometimes beat their wives, so I asked her if this were true. Without hesitation, she told me it is true. She added that Islam teaches women to be obedient to their husbands and, if a wife fails to do so, she could suffer a beating at the hands of her husband.

The question of polygamy also came up and she indicated that it is acceptable in some circumstances. For example, when a woman is infertile or unhealthy she may even encourage her husband to take another wife. Another qualifying reason for a man to take another wife is when there is no male child. A male heir is very important in Muslim life. Of course Muslim men can and do take on multiple wives without any of the above reasons.

Mai and other women she knew visited shrines of famous holy men in Islam. These shrines are scattered around Upper Sindh, some of them famous and others much less known. Women did not just visit on special occasions but anytime they wished. Taking garlands of flowers or sweets as offerings, they prayed at the shrines, beseeching the dead saint to intercede for them in whatever needs they had. They left a colorful silk scarf, tying it to a surrounding wall, a tree, or to his tomb.

Mai defended the custom of *purdah,* the practice in which females from puberty onward veil themselves from head to toe with a long flowing garment whenever they go outside their home. The type of *burka* the women wore varied widely, ranging from the one piece white cotton shuttle cock version she wore when she visited me to the more elaborate two-piece black nylon or rayon ones worn by more affluent urban women. She explained that men are men and *Allah* has made them the way they are. Whenever men see women without a *burka,* they have wrongful thoughts, even lust. Besides, no man would want another man looking at their own wives, sisters, daughters, or mothers. She found it difficult to understand why I did not wear a *burka.* She also enjoyed asking questions of her own about our customs, food, and family life.

Eventually, the time came for us to leave Shikarpur. We had lived there for about twelve years and felt as if we were a part of the community. *Mai* dropped by a few days before we were to leave. I explained our travel plans, telling her we would be taking an overnight train to Karachi, where we would spend a few days before boarding a huge plane that would take us home to America and our loved ones. She had questions about every aspect of the journey, and I explained to her how we were seated, served food, given blankets, and pillows for sleeping while in the plane.

She listened intently, taking in every word. Sitting cross-legged on the carpet she looked straight at me and said, with a big smile, "*Beyti,* when you get in the airplane, please fly over my house and salute me."

I wished with all my heart that I could grant her request. We embraced as we said farewell, close yet unlikely friends, knowing all the while our paths would never again cross and this was truly our last goodbye.

———

Not all my friends were Pakistani. Joan Holland, from England, was also very special. She had come out to what was then British India with her husband Ronnie, a medical doctor who specialized in eye diseases. Joan was a nurse as well as a skilled anesthetist. They were quite a team, both inside and outside the operating theater. Ronnie was a second generation missionary doctor, following in the footsteps of his illustrious father, Sir Henry Holland who had restored the sight of thousands of patients from across Sindh, Baluchistan and even Afghanistan. Taking over the hospital his father had established in the frontier town of Quetta, Ronnie served the population with love and compassion.

Joan and Ronnie arrived on the subcontinent as a newly married couple. They immersed themselves in the language and quickly earned the respect of those around them. Not long after arriving, while vacationing in Kashmir, Joan fell ill and was diagnosed with polio. Her husband was determined to defy the odds and save her life.

Desperately, he searched for ways to care for her. He found an old iron lung, rusty and unused. He had it cleaned up and placed Joan into the machine, manipulating the bellows by hand to keep her breathing.

All night he pressed the bellows, praying with every breath. Others surrounded the couple with prayer, including those in England where friends had been notified by telegram. Joan survived. As soon as she was able to travel, they returned to England for Joan's rehabilitation. Everyone thought the promising career in medical missions that Joan and Ronnie dreamed of had come to an abrupt end-everyone except Joan and Ronnie, that is. Determination and dedication took over and their faith in returning to the Indian subcontinent never wavered, despite the fact that Joan was paralyzed on one side from her waist down and would spend the rest of her life in a wheel chair.

As British India was granted independence and split into two countries in 1947, the Hollands found themselves back in Quetta serving in the newly-independent Pakistan. Because of its high altitude, the town was considered a hill station where people went during the summer months to escape the burning heat of the plains below. During the winter months, snow fell in Quetta and on the surrounding hills. Cold winds swept down into the city, making it difficult to keep the hospital open. Patients from surrounding areas found it difficult to travel over the snow-covered mountains. Some even migrated elsewhere during the winter months, seeking a warmer climate. Staff at the Quetta Mission Hospital also joined in this migration, relocating for up to three months in Shikarpur to conduct an extended annual eye camp.

By the time we arrived in Pakistan in the mid 1950's, the winter eye camp in Shikarpur had been going on for several years and had even developed into more permanent facilities. In fact, a fairly large compound had been built on the edge of town to house staff and care for patients. Between December and March, Dr. Holland and his colleagues conducted as many as three thousand eye surgeries. From time to time, doctors from the United States paid their way to Pakistan, helping in the heavy work load as well as gaining additional experience in cataract and other types of eye surgery.

We first met Joan and Ronnie in connection with their eye work in Shikarpur. Joan, dressed in a lovely crisp blouse and slacks, her short graying hair neatly combed, sat in a wheel chair, smiling and holding her hand out to welcome us into what was known as the Holland Bungalow, a modest building that served as their temporary home during the three months they lived in Shikarpur. It was a long structure, very simple and plain. Guests entered through a screened porch at the center. A group of rooms had been built on each side of this central area, each with a separate bath and each connected by a walkway. To some extent the Holland Bungalow looked like a rustic motel.

The large central living room was comfortable in a traditional British colonial style and was furnished with old but comfortable over-stuffed chairs and sofas, a few lamps, a scattering of pictures on the wall and a fraying rug covered most of the cement floor. A wide door at one end led to a dining area where a large wooden table took up most of the room. A kitchen with an old fashioned wood burning stove had been set up next to the dining room.

We sat in the parlor and were served a glass of juice. Other doctors who lived in the bungalow came into the room and we met each one. Joan and Ronnie were charming hosts, making everyone feel at home. A short while later, a servant appeared dressed in a white uniform and wearing a starched turban announced that dinner was ready. Joan directed us to our seats at the long table. Ronnie gave a brief blessing. As soon as we sat down, a servant appeared at my side with a bowl of piping hot soup, the first of several courses. I was being introduced to the English gentry. A salad course, fish, the main entrée and dessert followed. Afterwards, we all retired to the parlor for coffee and stimulating conversation.

During subsequent years, Joan and Ronnie as well as the visiting American doctors were often guests in our home. In many ways, the opening of the three-month Holland eye camp in Shikarpur became the highlight of the year for us. We enjoyed meeting the visiting American surgeons. One of them, a Dr. Bruchman from Connecticut, urged us to call him if we were ever visiting his part of the United States.

A couple of years later, when we returned to the United States for a year of furlough, we lived for several months in Hartford, Connecticut. Hu had enrolled in an Islamics study program at the Hartford Seminary. It was the first time that we had lived in New England. After settling into a tiny duplex in Newington, we gave Dr. Bruchman a call. He vividly remembered us and was delighted to hear from us. He wanted to know immediately if he could help us in our new situation. He even asked if we needed a car. Within a few days, his attractive wife came by with some goodies for the children. She also gave us tickets to the

New Britain Symphony, where we had the opportunity to hear the renowned pianist Andre Watts perform.

Later, we received an invitation to attend dinner at Dr. Bruchman's home. We were a bit apprehensive, but we accepted. A few days before the dinner, we drove by his address just to confirm the location. The house was large and luxurious from the outside. I wondered what we were getting ourselves into. We managed to find a baby sitter and set out on the evening of the dinner, entering a social circle which was new to us. A uniformed maid met us at the door and Mrs. Bruchman also met us. She introduced us to other guests, a professor from Harvard University and his teenage son.

Mrs. Bruchman was a charming hostess and put us at ease immediately. She told us that this was a full kosher meal. Before starting dinner, Dr. Bruchman said something I will always remember.

"Reverend Addleton, when visiting Shikarpur I will never forget the hospitality that you and others showed to me. Before every meal, someone also said a blessing. Will you please give us a prayer?"

I was amazed and I think that Hu was a little surprised. It was an honor to have been asked.

During the dinner conversation, Dr. Bruchman told us there were two things he especially remembered from his visit to Shikarpur. One was the selfless dedication Ronnie and Joan exemplified in their ministry to the blind. He mentioned the frayed rug in their living room at the Holland Bungalow and how unimportant material possessions were to them. The other memory was the evening he left by train from Shikarpur for Karachi to catch a plane for his return journey to the United States. It was a cold and windy night. We bundled up our children and took them to the train station to see Dr. Bruchman off. He was very moved by this gesture.

During our time in Hartford, Dr. Bruchman invited us to attend a doctor's meeting at the Hartford General Hospital as his guest. He introduced us to his medical colleagues as "my Baptist missionary friends." Later we received another dinner invitation. This time it was from the wife of a doctor who was involved in the Albert Schweitzer Medical Foundation.

On receiving this invitation I became a little anxious. We simply were not accustomed to moving in these circles and, of course, my first thought was what shall I wear? Hu took a day off from his studies to drive me around to all the dress shops in Hartford. The more I looked, the more stressed I became. Finally, I bought an attractive pink dress. However, when I returned home and tried it on again I was uncomfortable; it wasn't me and I just couldn't wear it. In my closet I had a lovely black dress that my mother who was an accomplished dressmaker, had sewed for me. She and I had gone around the stores in Macon, looking for a little black dress. Either they were not suitable or they were priced too high. In the end, we went to a fabric shop, picked out a pattern and some fine light weight woolen material. My mother made this simple black dress with a matching jacket and it cost a total of fifteen dollars.

My decision to wear that little black dress to the Hartford dinner party was the best decision I could have made. I felt elegant and very much at ease and we enjoyed the evening immensely.

When we walked into the reception room of the doctor's mansion, we were stunned to see such a large number of people. We were introduced to some of the leading personalities in Hartford, including not only doctors but also politicians, professors, and media personalities whose names were already familiar to us. Sipping ginger ale, we circulated around the room, working the crowd, each of us going our separate way. Tables had been set up in two large rooms. Hu was seated to the right of the hostess in one room and I to the right of the host in the other. It was a challenging and stimulating evening as we answered all kinds of questions about our work.

One very sophisticated young woman, recently returned from her studies at the Sorbonne in Paris, wanted to know why we would go to a distant country where people already had their religion and try to change them.

I answered her question with a question of my own: "Would you want to be born, grow up, live and die, and never hear of other alternatives?"

She thought for a moment and then answered, "No, I wouldn't."

"That is why we go." I replied, "To give them a choice."

It was a most interesting evening. By Christmas, Hu had finished his studies at Hartford Seminary and we returned to Macon, bringing an end to our brief encounters with high society soirees in New England.

Usually, Joan and Ronnie arrived in Shikarpur between Christmas and New Year's, enabling the hospital staff to celebrate with their families before moving temporarily to Sindh. One year, we invited the Hollands to come early, before the rest of the staff, and spend Christmas with us. They agreed and brought with them a Christmas tradition that has continued in our family to this day.

Ronnie insisted on bringing an English plum pudding as their contribution to our Christmas feast. Americans enjoy fruit cake and I always baked one. An English plum pudding is different: steamed, very rich and moist, and served with sauce, usually brandy sauce. Because of Joan's limited ability to cook while confined to a wheel chair, Ronnie was very capable in the kitchen. In fact, he had made the plum pudding he brought to dinner.

After the main course and before dessert, Ronnie excused himself and went to the kitchen. Moments later, he returned to our dining room with a flaming plum pudding. Our children loved it. Cutting into the pudding with a knife, there was another surprise—the knife hit hard metal. In keeping with English custom, he had thrown a coin into the batter and baked it with the pudding. Whoever found the coin could look forward to good luck throughout the New Year. We adopted this custom and, in later years, remember the Hollands every time we celebrate the holidays with a flaming pudding, sometimes with a coin baked inside.

One winter Joan became ill while in Shikarpur. Of course we wanted to help and I offered my services. Joan told me she'd like for me to shampoo her hair. We fixed a time and on another day I set out for the Holland Bungalow, preparing to respond to her request. How could I possibly shampoo Joan's hair? She was confined to a wheel chair, paralyzed on one side and had no use of her lower extremities.

I think Joan sensed my nervousness. She told me where to get towels, a basin, warm water, and the shampoo. She continued to tell me what to do. I draped a large towel around her shoulders and folded another one in her lap. Then I placed the wash basin in her lap and she bowed her head over the basin. I gently poured water over her head, applied shampoo, massaged her scalp, washed her hair, and rinsed it. Each time the basin filled, I emptied the water into the yard. We sat on the screened porch and the warm sunshine filtered through. When the shampooing was finished, I used my blow dryer to set her hair. She appreciated the results. Over and over, she assured me that she was not fragile, would not break and I should relax. That single incident fit Joan perfectly–even when enjoying a rare treat of her own, she was always thinking about others.

Every Sunday evening, along with other missionaries living in Shikarpur, we went to the Bungalow for Evensong. The order of service followed the *Anglican Book of Common Prayer*. One of the Baptist missionaries was asked to give a brief devotional talk. Joan always led in prayer. She had a collection of prayers, some of them her own and others drawn from other sources. They were heart-felt and we always left feeling blessed. At one point, Joan allowed me to read her personal prayer book, and I wish there had been some way to print it so others could have read them.

Having been introduced to an informal American pot-luck, the Hollands introduced the idea to the Sunday Evensongs they hosted. We brought casseroles, desserts, salads, and anything else easy to eat while standing up. On one occasion, we all looked on in disbelief as we opened our pots and pans–everyone, including the Hollands, had brought spaghetti.

The children, home from boarding school for winter break, added energy and enthusiasm to those Sunday gatherings. An adult prayed before dinner. Sometimes, these prayers became quite long and verbose. The children became fidgety; they were hungry and wanted to eat. Ronnie endeared himself to the children forever when he gave a short prayer of his own: "For every cup and plate full, make us truly grateful. Amen."

After many decades of service in Sindh and Baluchistan, Joan and Ronnie reached retirement age and returned to England. On his retirement, the Queen of England awarded him the OBE–Order of the British Empire–for his lifetime of service to Pakistan. In retirement, Joan and Ronnie bought a thatched roof cottage near Oxford University and set about renovating it. Special attention was given to building the kitchen cabinets, insuring that Joan could reach everything from her wheel chair. Always the enthusiastic gardener, Ronnie designed a beautiful flower garden that also included raspberry plants, herbs and other edibles. The retirement years, it appeared, provided an opportunity for more dreams to come true. Their children lived nearby. There were grandchildren to indulge.

We were living in Hyderabad when early one morning we turned our shortwave radio to BBC for news, a ritual that we had started many years before. Lying in bed and listening to the news, we heard the broadcaster inform his audience that "the wife of Dr. Ronnie Holland died in her sleep today."

Startled and saddened by the news, we thought of plans we had made to visit Joan and Ronnie on our way to the United States. They wanted us to see their cottage. Joan had been excited about our coming. Ronnie insisted we continue with our plans and so we did.

Ronnie greeted us warmly when we reached his lovely cottage. He gave us a glass of his homemade raspberry juice and showed us around the cottage and garden. We sat down to a lovely dinner, prepared entirely by Ronnie. He jumped up after every course and washed the dishes we had just used before serving the next course.

After dinner we talked for hours, reminiscing about our years together in Pakistan. We talked about Joan and how he had served her tea every day following her afternoon nap. One day he went upstairs with the tea tray, opened the bedroom door and found Joan dead. She had died peacefully in her sleep.

Devastated at first, by the time we arrived for our visit he appeared to have come to terms with her death. He was not only coping but continued to be involved in various types of volunteer medical work and other services.

At one point during our visit we told Ronnie that we wanted to set a time when we could lay some flowers on Joan's grave.

"Joan is among the roses in our garden," he replied. At her request, her body had been cremated and her ashes spread in the garden outside the cottage she loved.

Ronnie arranged a marvelous program for us in England. We attended an ancient Norman church on Sunday morning and met the editor of the *London Times* who worshipped there. Ronnie was a lay reader in that church as well as others in the vicinity. He asked Hu to deliver the sermon that morning. He took us out to the White Horse Downs and presented me with a lovely pin from there. We also visited the ruins of an old church at Glastonbury where tradition has it that

King Arthur and his knights met at the round table. We drove through the Robin Hood woods and to Stonehenge. In those days, Stonehenge had not yet been fenced and we were able to move freely among the stone monuments.

One lovely warm and sunny day, Ronnie packed a picnic basket and we sat on a blanket laid out on the grass. He rolled out a table cloth and a lunch of cheese, pate, bread and fresh fruit along with a thermos of hot tea. Carefully pulling out the dishes, Ronnie laid out fine china and silver cutlery. Joan would have planned it just that way.

Again, we recalled the many precious memories of our times together in Shikarpur. For some reason, I remembered that Hu had once asked Joan if, when she dreamed, she was paralyzed in her dreams.

Joan's reply had been immediate and emphatic: "No, in my dreams. I am not in a wheel chair. I am always running and dancing."

Ronnie and Joan both danced through our lives and left a lasting impression. Their friendship enriched our lives, and we became better people because of them.

Bettie Rose, 1948

Our Shikarpur home

Village Oxcart

Tonga

Worship with Christian woman

Rockedge, Murree home and birthplace of Jonathan and Nancy

Bettie wearing a *duputta*

Bettie wearing a saree

Painted truck

Mari Wari village women

Bus loaded with passengers

Bible Translation Committee

David on a train

Family on vacation in the mountains

Hu & Bettie enjoying afternoon tea at Lintott's

Entertaining

Our 50th Wedding Anniversary with family

Human powered rickshaw

Chapter Seven

WEST MEETS EAST

We always enjoyed traveling to and from Pakistan by ship during the 1950's and early 1960's. Our first trip across the Atlantic had been by freighter. Another one, five years later, was on the *Queen Elizabeth*. This route took us from New York to South Hampton in England. The opportunity to travel on the historic *Queen Elizabeth* represented the height of luxury for us.

We were assigned a spacious cabin in the tourist section. The food was excellent and many recreation opportunities were available on board. Special provisions had been made for children, including a fully equipped playroom supervised by nannies. David, Nancy, and Jonathan enjoyed the games, movies, and toys as well as the opportunity to spend time with other children.

On arrival in England, we took a train to Liverpool. From there, we sailed for Pakistan on the Anchor Line, a well known shipping company that for many years had sailed ships from England to India and other countries in the Far East. This leg was the longest part of our voyage, and we were assigned two small, cramped rooms located around the corner from each other. It was warm by the time we reached the Mediterranean and became even hotter as we traveled further east.

One of the most enjoyable aspects of ship travel was meeting other passengers. I noticed quite a large number of young English women traveling to India. As I became more acquainted with them, I found out that they had met and married their Prince Charming back in England

and were on their way east to visit the place where their husbands had grown up. A number of them would be meeting their in-laws for the first time.

Most of the women were very excited. Some had toddlers with them. However, one of the women was not excited at all. She was apprehensive about her future and actually became physically ill. She kept the ship's doctor busy with her various ailments. Often she called him at night when she couldn't sleep. Her agitation and anxiety were obvious.

I have often wondered about this young woman and what became of her. Little did I realize that during the coming years I would meet many American and European women who had married handsome young Pakistani Muslims. Their stories were sometimes unbelievable.

—

I will never forget the young woman from California who showed up for an Easter Service at the International Church in Karachi. She was about twenty-one years old. Hu was serving as pastor of the church at that time.

She told us briefly that she had arrived only a week or so before and had heard about the English speaking congregation. She hadn't expected to meet other Americans. She was Catholic and had been married in a Catholic church back in California. Her husband, she said, had participated in the pre-marriage counseling required by the church and had even converted to Catholicism. The pictures in her large and beautiful wedding album confirmed her story.

About two months after the wedding her husband returned to Pakistan alone. She remained in the United States to obtain necessary documents for entering Pakistan. He was an only son and lived with his widowed mother and sister together in an apartment. Ordinarily the arrival of a new bride would have prompted a big party to introduce the newlywed couple to family and friends. However, nothing of the sort had been planned. In fact, she arrived to find a rather cool reception from her mother-in-law and sister-in-law. He would leave her in the evenings to join his male friends for tea, movies or whatever. From the very beginning, she was expected to play a passive role and was excluded from any decision making.

She wore jeans and tee shirts like her contemporaries would have worn back in California. Young married women did not wear these in Pakistan, at least not in public. She did not know the language spoken by the women in the household. She knew no one and was utterly alone. Attending an Easter service provided an opportunity to meet with others who would receive her warmly.

After the service, she asked if she could come again and talk with us. Of course she could come anytime. She returned a couple of days later, this time with a packed bag. She had left her husband, she said, because he had told her that he did not love her. He did not want to touch her. According to her, they had not been intimate since her arrival in Pakistan. In her sorrow, she said she could not understand how her husband could have changed so drastically in the few weeks they had been separated. She begged Hu to talk with him and try to get them reconciled.

The handsome young husband agreed to discuss the situation and came to our home. We had not met him before. Hu took him into his office and the two of them talked behind closed doors. I went with the young woman upstairs and we tried to talk. She mostly wept. She told me over and over again the story of how they met, how they dated, the fun they had with their friends, the love her family had for him, and their beautiful wedding. Now, all her dreams for the future seemed to have ended. We prayed together and I offered her tea.

Eventually, my husband called for me to come downstairs. I could tell by the expression on his face the news was bad. He told me, "The marriage is over." The young man was not interested in trying to put it back together. Perhaps the cultural and religious obstacles were stronger than he had realized, and he just could not make the change needed for a true partnership. Moreover, his mother had refused to accept his new wife.

I wondered if there was another possibility. Perhaps a young Pakistani girl had been chosen for him, and the arrival of a new bride from America had disrupted those plans. Who really knew what was going on in his head when he left Pakistan, started a new life in California, and returned home to face reality? One certain fact: this was the end of a very short marriage. Thankfully, children were not a factor.

While accepting that the marriage was over, Hu did not believe the husband should be let off so easily. He told the young man he should telephone his father-in-law in the United States and tell him exactly what he had just related. He called from our house. Hu also required him to arrange an immediate flight for his wife's return to California and the loving family who awaited her. We helped get her things together for the midnight flight. She was concerned about the Church's acceptance of her as a divorcee. We promised to write to the Pope if necessary in support of the annulment she planned to request.

Several months later, we received a letter from her. Enclosed was a photo showing a smiling young woman. In the letter she expressed her thanks and appreciation to us for helping her through her ordeal. She was on the way to rebuilding her life.

—

Early one morning we had a call from another young American woman whom we had met on several occasions. Thin and downcast, she rarely smiled. Surprisingly, she had a part-time job. She also had children. She and her family lived with her mother-in-law who watched her every move. Whenever she wanted to leave the house, she first had to obtain permission from her mother-in-law. When making a request, she had to describe exactly where she was going and when she would return. For all practical purposes, she felt like a prisoner in her own house.

As is common in most upper-middle class Pakistani households, the several household servants included a driver. The driver took her shopping, to her part-time job, and wherever else she had to go. The driver also dropped the children at their private school and took them home afterwards. He kept the mother-in-law informed of every place her daughter-in-law went.

The young woman was deeply unhappy with her situation and wanted out. She thought of taking the children and leaving. However, when searching for passports and other documents she discovered they had all been destroyed. Confiding her story to officers at the American Consulate, she was able to obtain new passports which were safely kept at the Consulate. Her mother back in the United States had secretly remitted money for the day she could leave.

Her request to us seemed simple enough. Unable to use the telephone in her home without someone listening, she wanted our help in obtaining a schedule of flights leaving Karachi during working hours. Because her husband had influence, she wanted to make sure she was traveling on a flight that did not stop off in any nearby Muslim country. She was afraid, she said, that when her husband found her missing she would be apprehended the moment the plane landed.

Taking these fears into account, she had put together a well-thought out plan. After collecting her passports, money and the children she would then proceed to the airport by taxi and hop on a plane to freedom.

This was a difficult situation and we were sympathetic. However, we found it impossible to go along with her plan. In any case, most international flights left Karachi at night, and there were no planes leaving during daylight hours that fit her needs. We suggested that, unless violence and abuse were taking place, she should wait for a few months at which time she would be allowed to visit her parents in the United States. On arrival, she should consult a lawyer and go from there.

Conceding to this approach, she emphasized her love for her husband and said she could live with him in America. She found it suffocating to live in a traditional joint family system in which the mother-in-law ruled. She and her husband and their children had their own bedrooms, but other brothers with their wives and children also lived in the large house. Servants cleaned, cooked, and took care of the children. However, married life for this young American in a large and upper class Pakistani family did not turn out to be the storybook dream she had imagined. After several years in Pakistan, she wanted the American Dream: her own house with a white picket fence and the liberty to express herself in her own home. She enjoyed her part-time job, but it did not give her the outlet she needed.

We did not hear from the young woman for some time. Later, we learned she had left to visit her parents during the summer and never returned. I don't know if her husband joined her or if the marriage ended. We never saw her again.

For several years, in the mid 1970's, we lived in Hyderabad, a city of culture and history situated on the Indus River between Shikarpur and Karachi. It was much larger than Shikarpur and considerably more open and cosmopolitan. I enjoyed the relative freedom, including the opportunity to meet people from many walks of life and without the restrictions I faced when living in the more conservative culture of Upper Sindh. I was able to shop the bazaars more frequently. It was more fun going with another woman rather than depending on my husband. Since a large number of foreigners worked and lived in the area, I was not singled out for unwanted stares from men. Even local Muslim women appeared less restricted and I saw a few of them going about without the *burka*.

Our circle of friends in Hyderabad included army officers, doctors, government officials, and members of the local business community. As always, I spent more time with the wives. One was an American married to a Pakistani doctor, another a European woman married to a colonel in the Pakistan Army.

Both women had spent many years in Pakistan. Their children were older than mine and had been raised as Muslims. Islam allows a man to marry Christians and Jews, who are considered "people of the book." In such cases, the wife is not required to convert to Islam, though this sometimes happens, especially if family pressure is brought on the new wife. A Muslim wedding ceremony is certainly required for without it children born to the couple would be considered illegitimate.

Neither of my friends considered themselves Muslim. On the contrary, they often talked about their Christian faith. They would sometimes attend Easter and Christmas services in local churches.

One Christmas we invited both families to join us for Christmas dinner. I loved the holidays and always prepared the best feast possible. Throughout the year, I kept my eyes open for goodies I would normally not expect to find in the bazaar, hiding them for safe keeping until I brought them out for the holidays.

I often served lamb at Christmas, making it the centerpiece of our dinner table. An American friend had given us a canned ham for Christmas. When I invited our friends for dinner, I asked the women if their husbands would object if I served ham. In deference to our neighbors, we almost never ate pork. But this was a small celebration among friends and perhaps on this occasion it would be permissible. I was thinking in particular of these two western women living in Hyderabad who probably rarely if ever enjoyed ham.

"Of course, that would be fine," my friends replied when I asked about the ham. After all, their husbands had traveled extensively and were very tolerant.

Pulling out all the stops, I was determined to make the best Christmas dinner ever. The table setting reflected this and included a variety of fresh vegetables, salads, homemade breads and rolls, several desserts, fruit and nuts. A perfectly roasted leg of lamb took center stage. Off to one side I placed the small ham, garnished with sliced pineapple. I was surprised when I noticed that neither of the women touched the ham. However, their husbands ate it and even went back for seconds.

This reaction of the wives as well as their husbands perplexed me. Occasionally, I had heard a very Westernized Pakistani say that they were half Muslim, meaning they drank wine but did not eat pork. Ordinarily, eating ham is the last taboo to go—but, on this occasion, the two men really seemed to enjoy eating ham.

Both women appeared to be happy and content. Their children struggled to find their identity, especially the girls. They were not required to wear the *burka* as their Muslim counterparts. Yet, other social restrictions applied. For example, they could not interact with boys nor go about alone. Children of this particular American mother eventually returned to the States for their education, stayed and probably had a choice in their marriage. Children of the European mother chose to remain in Pakistan and loosely followed local customs regarding marriage.

I picked up on a number of concerns expressed in the many conversations I had with foreign women married to local men. One European woman, deeply religious, had wanted her children taught the Christian faith. However, she was not allowed to take them to church. Thus, bath time became an opportunity for her to tell them about her own faith and beliefs.

Another woman, very beautiful and very well adjusted to the life she had chosen for herself, expressed her concern to me about the type of funeral she would have. If she died in Pakistan, she was afraid she would be given a Muslim burial. She was a Christian and wanted to be buried according to Christian funeral rites. She worried about this for a long time. One day she told me she had resolved her fear of dying in Pakistan and being given a Muslim funeral rite. She referred to a verse from the Bible on death which stated that "to be absent from the body is to be present with God." After reading this, she said to me, "It doesn't matter what is done to my body when I die, I will be with God."

Karachi is a large metropolitan city. Over the years, we saw it grow from about a million people when we arrived in the mid 1950's to about 10 million when we departed nearly four decades later. The current estimation is about 17 million.

The city's diversity is reflected in its social life. People come from all over the world. Since women's clubs abound, there are opportunities to meet and socialize with others from a similar background.

The American Women's Club was one such organization. In addition to providing a series of social events, it also encouraged women to become involved in the life of the community. Reaching out to the various charity organizations in the city as well as country wide brought the women together in fund raising as well as hands-on ventures.

One of the biggest annual social events was the Christmas Ball. It was always well attended and the American women married to Muslim Pakistani men came out in large numbers. Their husbands enjoyed the celebration as much as anyone. They seemed to like dressing up and their wives sparkled in beautiful and stunning formal outfits. The dinner menu was always typically American. Far from home, American women who had decided to spend their lives in Pakistan enjoyed the warmth of sharing the special season with other Americans as well as with their Pakistani husbands.

Inconsistent as it may have been, alcoholic beverages were always available at these large social events. Both the American women and their Muslim husbands enjoyed the drinks. Alcohol is forbidden in Islam and is not ordinarily for sale. Except that is, for Christians. There are special shops for them. With government permits, small quantities can be legally purchased. Cost alone prohibits buying for most people. Diplomats and foreign business people are allowed to import limited quantities, also contributing to a black market in alcohol sales. Occasionally, we would be invited to homes of business tycoons for special events. Imagine our surprise to find fully stocked bars with alcohol flowing. Confirmed teetotalers, we navigated among the guests who represented nearly every nationality and interest.

—

Over the years, we met many Western women married to Pakistani Muslim men. Occasionally we met a few Western men who married Pakistani Muslim women. These marriages are much less common, largely because of the Islamic religious principle that a Muslim man may marry outside the faith while no such provision exists for Muslim women.

We did attend one such wedding when a young and handsome American man fell in love with a beautiful Pakistani woman from a strict Muslim family. They worked for the same company. In traditional Pakistani society, there is no custom for dating. However, in a large city like Karachi there were opportunities for men and women to meet at socially mixed events. In this way, the couple became acquainted with each other. The young man decided to leave his Catholic faith and convert to Islam. This was the only way such a mixed marriage could find favor with her family. The wedding was huge and the bride and groom, dressed in traditional clothing, made a handsome and seemingly happy couple.

Other West-East marriages also come to mind, some of them involving Christians. I remember one lovely English girl who fell in love with a Pakistani Christian. He was a leader in the community, and they both found their niche in areas of service, raising a family and becoming a model for a happy home life.

I also recall an American Christian girl who fell in love with a Christian Pakistani in the United States. They married and both of them traveled back and forth to Pakistan. He was well educated and found employment with above average income. She loved Pakistan and her in-laws. Soon, they had children and were living the middle class American dream.

At the same time, the couple had to reckon with other factors. The husband was the eldest son. This status in Pakistani culture brings responsibilities for an extended family that most American couples never encounter.

His mother was a widow with other children still at home and his financial responsibility for them was mandatory. His income, sufficient for his small growing American family, was stretched to its limit. Regular remittances had to be sent to the husband's extended family back in Pakistan. Moreover, arrangements had to be made to ensure that the sisters back in Pakistan were properly married. Weddings are expensive and the bride's family is expected to bear most of the costs.

Trips to and from Pakistan added to the increasing financial burden for the couple. Tensions were inevitable and the couple sought counseling. Over time, the couple became more aware of the vast differences in their respective cultures and worked hard to overcome them. For example, one problem in particular was that in Pakistani families, children often sleep with their parents. The couple's daughters were approaching adolesence and the American wife felt uncomfortable with this. She wanted it stopped.

Another area of conflict emerged when he asserted dominance over her. Women in Pakistan do face the issue of inequality. My American friend was out-spoken, assertive and found it difficult to tolerate what she termed his control.

Their common faith and good intentions were not enough to bridge the divide and they ultimately divorced. Perhaps not surprisingly, the tug-of-war as it relates to their children and in-laws continues.

—

A caveat in a Christian-Muslim marriage, while not common, sometimes surfaces. A Muslim man may exercise his right to marry another wife.

One evening we received a telephone call from a young American woman asking us to visit her friend who had been hospitalized. Upon arriving, we learned the patient had been admitted with an overdose of sleeping pills. She and her husband had been married for a number of years. The marriage appeared happy and durable except for one thing - so far, there had been no children.

Like Sara in the Old Testament, this American woman wanted her husband to have a child, preferably a son. They had discussed this for a very long time and the wife concluded that the husband she loved should indeed take another wife, one who would bear him children. Finally, arrangements were made and the day for the wedding arrived. The reality of sharing her husband was too much, filling her with more dread than even the prospect of death itself. Only the quick thinking and intervention of close friends who saw what was happening saved her life. They took her to the hospital.

Another Western woman I met was not bothered at all when her husband took another wife. Long before she entered his life, a distant cousin had been chosen for him. Especially among Sindh's landlord class, it is not unusual for men of importance to marry women from their ancestral village. Sometimes such marriages involve cousins. In fact, former Prime Minister Zulfikar Ali Bhutto whose family owned thousands of acres in Upper Sindh had contracted such a marriage, marrying both his cousin who lived in the ancestral village as well as Nusrat, a much more sophisticated and educated woman whose family had originally come from Iran.

An American woman we knew had married into a similar situation. Indeed, she lived her entire married life knowing that her husband had married his cousin, not because he was in love with her but to fulfill a family obligation. He maintained two households, one in Karachi and the other in his rural ancestral village. He had children with both wives. If there were problems, no one ever knew it. The American wife was loved and beloved by her husband and his family. For her part, she understood the situation and had adjusted to it. In fact, she encouraged her husband to bring his village sons to the city for quality education. She treated them as her own. Her children called them cousins.

Reflecting on these many relationships, I can't help but think of the saying of Rudyard Kipling "Oh East is east and West is west and never the twain shall meet." In Pakistan, the two did meet, sometimes successfully and sometimes not. Under the circumstances, misunderstandings were inevitable, often at great personal cost of those directly involved. It was never my role to make judgments about what was right and what was wrong in any particular relationship. Instead, I simply was there to share in the struggles and joys of these women whose lives became

119

woven into the fabric of my own as we both experienced what it was like to live in Pakistan.

Chapter Eight

CHILDBIRTH DRAMA

Our son David was only sixteen months old when we left Macon for Pakistan. Both Hu and I come from large families. I was one of eight children and my husband had twelve siblings. We hoped David would also grow up with brothers and sisters. Living in Pakistan would present special challenges. Nonetheless, we looked forward to the time when our dream of another child would become reality.

We had been in Pakistan for just over seven months, having arrived in May of 1956. Following language training in Murree in the mountains to the north, we had settled into our new Ratodero home. The locals referred to it as a town but, in reality, it was little more than a village.

We lived in a kiln-dried brick house next to another missionary family, Ralph and Polly Brown. We each had our own small courtyard. The house had a flat roof for sleeping and we slept there during the hot season.

During the day, David and I would go up to the roof and look down upon life around us. My husband was not allowed on the roof during daylight hours since women in neighboring courtyards could be seen.

The streets of Ratodero were narrow and cobblestone. In fact, standing in the middle of a street it was sometimes possible to stretch out our arms and touch the houses on each side. The town generator shut down during the day. At night, electricity was available sporadically, providing enough power to light a single light bulb hanging from the ceiling in each room as well as a small fan. Everything we experienced was new and exciting. We didn't want to miss a thing around us.

One day, during the middle of language study, I heard the haunting sound of a flute, coming from the outside of our walled courtyard.

"Where is that coming from?" I asked my tutor.

We both looked outside and saw a snake charmer. We had heard about these men who charmed the deadly cobra. Sometimes, they carried a mongoose in a basket, staging mock fights between the cobra and the one adversary that could almost always defeat them, something that Rudyard Kipling had written about.

The entire household went out to watch. Neighbors joined in. My husband reached for his camera. David, by now approaching his second birthday, jumped with excitement, tinged with just a little fear.

Suddenly, an old wrinkled and toothless woman appeared in front of me. Excited and alarmed, she physically pushed me away. I was totally taken aback and even angry that she dared to push me and order me back into my own house.

Other women were jostling in front of me, covered in shawls or *burkas* with only their eyes showing. I, too, was modestly clothed with my head covered and wearing a long dress with sleeves. What could I be doing wrong? The snake charmer continued with his music and others watched with interest and amusement.

I was disturbed. I still didn't know enough Sindhi to find out just what was going on around me. Hu asked our cook to explain. He hedged, telling us that it was just a local custom.

We gave the snake charmer some small change and went back inside. Then Hu began to quiz the cook more closely.

"*Sahib*, this woman says that *memsahib* has a baby in her stomach," he said. "She is warning *memsahib* that if she looks upon the snake, it will be very bad. Harm will come to both *memsahib* and the baby," he continued.

We wanted a baby but this came as news to us. We laughed it off as an amusing and even ridiculous episode.

A few weeks later I needed medical attention for a minor ailment. I visited an Australian missionary doctor in Sukkur, a town on the

Indus River about forty miles away. She informed me that I was in fact pregnant and the baby was due the following June.

———

The next months moved slowly. Except for a little morning sickness, I kept well. Dr. Maybel Bruce, our new mission doctor who specialized in obstetrics, arrived from Massachusetts. She lived nearby. This birth would be her first delivery outside a modern, well-equipped American hospital. In late spring, as the hottest part of the year approached, we departed by train for Murree along with Dr. Bruce and other missionary families.

Our first home in Murree had been Sunshine Villa. During our second summer, we stayed in a complex of apartments known as Rockedge. It was a fitting name because the houses were built on a rocky ridge facing toward Kashmir. Our house was more or less in the middle of all the others. There were windows all around and the view toward the mountains was spectacular.

Often, we took our language lessons outside. The cool mountain air was refreshing and invigorating. In the distance, we could see the snow covered mountains of the Pir Panjal rising above Srinagar in Indian-held Kashmir. The bazaar was just a short distance down the ridge. From time to time we stopped at a lovely tea shop called Lintott's, enjoying afternoon tea with a coconut macaroon or a spicy *samosa*. At other times, we walked in the other direction toward the pine forests surrounding Kashmir Point. When the weather was good, it was as if we could see forever. When the monsoons approached, we would be enveloped in thick mist and clouds.

Traveling merchants sometimes visited us at home, including fruit and vegetable peddlers, the flower man with his gorgeous flowers in a straw basket and the bakery peddler who opened a tin trunk to show off his delicious pastries. Even a jewel peddler came around from time to time, displaying his precious stones of every shape and kind. I once bought an opal from one of these peddlers, setting it in a ring that I still enjoy wearing to this day.

Family life was good in Murree. We followed a more predictable schedule and our diet of fresh fruits and vegetables along with the fresh air kept us in good health. We attended a community church populated by missionaries living throughout Pakistan who, like us, had escaped to the hills during the hot summer season. The church, one of the first buildings constructed when the British discovered Murree in the mid-nineteenth century, was located down the hill and at the edge of the bazaar.

We walked down the mountain to Holy Trinity Church each Sunday, often hiring a donkey to carry David. Representing countries and missions from around the world, we experienced something like heaven below in our relationships and involvements with each other. To this day, we maintain contact with many of the people we met, linking our past and present in ways that provide continuity with some of the best years of our life.

Asian flu was making its way around the world in the summer of 1957. I woke up one Sunday morning feeling achy and weak. At my urging, Hu took David and the two of them made their way down the hill for Sunday school and church. I was surprised but relieved when they returned a bit early. I was glad to see them because I had developed a fever. My temperature registered at 105 degrees.

Hu got wet towels and put them over my body in an effort to bring the fever down. This and medication helped. But I continued to feel poorly the next day. I was not eating. Hu had made ice cream, thinking that would help. We did not have a refrigerator so he churned the ice cream the old fashioned way. I appreciated his efforts and managed to eat a small serving.

Afterwards, I developed a violent chill. When I managed to get warm with layers of blankets, my temperature reached 106 degrees. Dr. Bruce sent for ice and covered my burning body with cold, wet towels. She also sent for Dr. Hamm, another missionary doctor. He came immediately. He brought with him some ice cubes and tea. His was one of the few families living on the hillside with a refrigerator. His wife Lucy had insisted he bring these items along – a thoughtful gesture bringing relief to my parched mouth.

Other than the glass of iced tea, I remember little of what was happening around me. Dr. Hamm diagnosed malaria rather than the flu. He prescribed a dose of quinine. He also said labor would now very likely begin as quinine often induced labor in pregnant women. I kept asking him over and over, "Will the baby be all right, will the baby be all right?"

Dr. Hamm never answered me directly, but assured me that I would be okay. Later, he returned to his home on the other side of the mountain.

The first mild contractions began shortly after nine in the evening. Hu dozed on the sofa. Dr. Bruce lay down next to me in our bed. Connie Johnson, a registered nurse and a colleague who had two boys of her own, came to assist. She lay down on a cot in David's room. Nothing happened, other than occasional contractions and dull discomfort which later turned to a sharp, continuous pain.

Dr. Bruce got up about two in the morning, examined me and thought I was in good labor. Hu awoke and helped Dr. Bruce set up our bedroom for the pending delivery.

Our bed was a wooden frame strung with rope and a thick cotton mattress that required frequent fluffing. It was also quite low to the floor. The dining room table, more solid, higher, and firm, was pulled into the bedroom. A thin mattress covered it. The dining table became a delivery table.

Dr. Bruce and Hu made coffee and Connie got up to join them. Connie stood beside me with a trylene mask which she put on my face during each contraction. She told me when to breathe and when to push. Hu stood on the other side, holding my hand, giving encouragement and reassurance.

Progress was slow, even after Dr. Bruce cut the membrane. Around four in the morning, the baby's head became visible and those in attendance got excited. I was hopeful it would all be over soon. Much to our dismay, Dr. Bruce discovered the baby's head was coming posterior. She tried her best to turn the baby with her hands and then forceps.

After a long while, the baby's head had not presented. It seemed to come out half-way a couple of times but then popped back inside. Both Connie and Dr. Bruce continued to check the baby's heart. I was scared because once Connie was unable to find a heart beat. I was given a sedative but got little relief from the terrible pain. Despite Dr. Bruce's best efforts, her first delivery in Pakistan was turning into a nightmare. Again she sent for Dr. Hamm, who lived in a hillside cottage a few miles away.

My husband later told me after she sent for Dr. Hamm, Dr. Bruce sat on a stool at the foot of the table, bowed her head and prayed. She asked God for help. Her prayer was heard because the baby turned and the head came out, followed by the whole body. It was a boy. He cried. He was alive.

Connie took charge of the baby, cleaning him up and measuring and weighing him. Dr. Bruce waited for the placenta to expel. Dr. Hamm arrived and still the placenta had not come. Dr. Bruce tried to bring it out and then Dr. Hamm put on his gloves and tried until he was able to remove it. The pain throughout this ordeal was excruciating.

I was moved from the dining room table to my bed and eventually managed to fall asleep. Connie helped clean up and went home to her family. She had been up all night. Dr. Bruce lay down on the couch near the baby to sleep and Hu went into David's room. The baby whom we had named Jonathan Stuart also slept. I was more peaceful and pain free than I had been in days.

Sometime later, I was suddenly awakened by strange sensations on my back. I turned and saw several tiny pink creatures in my bed. They had been running up and down my spine.

I stood up in the bed and screamed in what must have been a really loud and alarming voice. Dr. Bruce came running simply aghast at what she was seeing. Hu came from the other direction, alarm showing on his face. Suddenly I was speechless, and all I could do was point to my bed. There were four or five very tiny pink, hairless mice nestled in my bed. They must have had the same birthday as our son and the mother must have been in labor along with me in the attic of our home. These little creatures had literally fallen through the cracks.

———

Already, my first delivery in Pakistan had involved enough drama to last a lifetime. But there was more yet to come.

Dr. Bruce had arrived in Pakistan with some of the latest equipment in her sea freight. And, she was proud to tell us, a clamp needed to circumcise our newborn son was in the freight. She declared it a safe and simple procedure. We could watch if we wanted to. She also mentioned that it was bloodless.

On a bright and sunny afternoon a few days after the dramatic birth of Jonathan, Dr. Bruce decided it was time for the circumcision. Our dining room table had already served as a delivery table; now it would be transformed into an operating table. We placed the table near the windows where there was plenty of light. She applied the tiny little clamp and then cut the skin. The baby did not make a sound, though I noticed a little drop of blood. I remembered the doctor had said the procedure would be bloodless, so I wondered about the oozing.

We went to bed early. Around eleven that night we heard a knock at the door. Dr. Bruce was standing outside. She wanted to check on Jonathan. The site of the circumcision continued to ooze blood. Dr. Bruce took a needle and thread and sterilized it in a sauce pan set on top of our kerosene stove. Minutes later, she took a stitch or perhaps two and told us not to worry.

Now, I began to really worry.

Next morning was Sunday. Our neighbors had already left for church. I had insisted that Hu and David go as well; assuring them I would be fine. And I was. The time alone passed quickly.

While enjoying the beautiful sunny day and looking out the window, I saw Dr. Bruce coming up the hill, almost running. She was alone. She came directly to our apartment. Again, she took a sauce pan and this time sterilized a syringe. She was not much of a talker when she was doing what she did best—taking care of her patients. But I wanted to know what was going on.

While she was sitting in church, she could not get her mind off Jonathan and the fact that he continued to bleed. Suddenly, she remembered it was routine in the United States to give mothers Vitamin K during labor. It was supposed to help clot the blood. Leaving church early, she had stopped at a chemist to buy a syringe and a vial of Vitamin K. She then proceeded immediately to Rockedge. Sure enough, after injecting Jonathan with the vitamin, the bleeding stopped. However, even this incident was not the end of our continuing family drama.

Later, Jonathan turned yellow. When the jaundice continued, the missionary medical personnel once again became concerned. A lab technician was called to check his blood each day. Although I did not know it at the time, apparently there was speculation among the medical personnel that perhaps the two of us should be taken out of

127

the country for more comprehensive testing. Somehow, we managed to get through the crisis and before long we had a healthy and thriving little one.

The day Jonathan was born, the gardener at Rockedge brought me a large bouquet of beautiful dahlias. He congratulated Hu profusely on the birth of our second son. He emphasized how good Allah was to bless us with boys.

The baby was very active, keeping us awake during some nights. However, our worries were now largely gone. We returned to Ratodero in the fall. I was more than proud to show the baby to our neighbors and friends. Jonathan was as fair and blond as he could be. Everyone wanted to see and touch him. They had never seen such fair skin.

I was especially glad to show Jonathan to the toothless and wrinkled old woman who had told me of his conception even before I knew it myself. I did not, however, tell her the drama surrounding his birth nor the events that placed both him and his mother in serious danger.

After the birth, Dr. Hamm reminded me of the question that I had kept asking him throughout the delivery, "Will the baby be all right, and will the baby be all right?"

"I never answered you," he said, "because, under such circumstances, it is hardly ever all right, either for the mother or for the baby."

—

One of my local friends was having her first baby. She was young and a newlywed and as a rule, newlyweds don't wait around for procreation to begin. It is important for all to know that the marriage has been consummated and that both the young groom and bride are very capable of reproduction. In Islamic societies, failure to produce a child and especially a male child sometimes results in the husband taking on a second wife.

Family planning, then a new concept in Pakistan, was frowned upon. One of my friends, a woman doctor, told me that only the rich and educated could afford family planning. She was deeply concerned about this because she could see her beloved country becoming overly populated. I still remember the time in the late nineteen fifties or early nineteen sixties when a massive nation wide family planning campaign was launched. It involved condom distribution and offered either radios or cash for any man or woman who agreed to be sterilized. From time to time, we could see condoms, blown up like balloons, floating around the countryside.

Traditionally, Islam is kind to an expectant woman and pregnancies are welcomed. Along with sick and nursing mothers, an expectant mother is exempt from the daily fast during the month of Ramadan.

The actual fast begins just before dawn and ends at sundown with the evening prayer. Public announcements remind the faithful at the beginning and end of each day when to start and finish their fast. During our years in Sindh, a siren from the fire station was often used to make the announcement. In earlier days, the shooting of a canon informed the people. Nowdays an electric amplifier makes the call.

Living at close quarters with our neighbors in Ratodero, we were always awakened in the predawn hours by the banging of cooking utensils on our street. The women got up early to prepare the pre-fast meal.

The Islamic calendar is a lunar one and the timing of Ramadan is moved up by a couple of weeks each year. Sometimes, it comes during the short winter days. At other times, it falls during the long, hot summer months. Regardless of the time of year, during Ramadan all faithful Muslims abstain from eating, drinking and smoking throughout the daylight hours. Sexual intercourse is also prohibited. Antisocial behavior such as envy, stealing, quarrelling, and lying is condemned.

Weddings are not held during Ramadan. During the advanced stages of pregnancy, a man is not allowed sexual intercourse nor is it permitted for the first forty days after childbirth or until bleeding stops. Couples are also admonished to show restraint during the time when the mother is nursing.

My young friend asked me to sit with her when she delivered her first born. Although I had given birth to two sons, I had never seen a birth. Our first born, David, was delivered in a hospital in Macon. Everything was programmed and I was not really aware of anything from the time I was admitted until I was in my room and was told, "It's a boy." By contrast, the birth of our second son, Jonathan, had been painfully dramatic.

I was delighted when asked to hold my friend's hand during her own delivery. The room was dimly lit and Parveen lay on the low, rope-strung bed. She was in pain and more than a little scared. Small children ran in and out of the room. A cat slept nearby and, just outside the door, a dog came and went, sometimes barking. There was no running water. A single bare light bulb hung from the ceiling. Female relatives sat around cross-legged on mats.

While holding her hand, I assured Parveen all would be well. A midwife, known locally as a *dai*, was present. Home deliveries involving midwives were very much the norm. Some had training and most had experience. A birth is considered a normal part of life. Fortunately, most births do turn out to be normal. Nonetheless, I heard stories about some of the severe complications which mothers faced in Pakistan. Some even died in childbirth at the hands of an untrained or incompetent *dai*.

Government-run hospitals were available in some places. It was often difficult if not impossible to attract skilled female doctors to live in the more remote and isolated areas. In any case, a man would typically prefer to see his wife dead than to have a male doctor take care of her. I remember once when one of our own missionary women suffered a miscarriage. She continued to bleed as she was being transported to a mission hospital many miles away. Her condition became critical and it was decided she should go immediately to the nearest government hospital. A male doctor on duty saved her life, and we were all grateful for his professional skills and care. Very probably, it was one of the few occasions in which he had attended a female patient.

As I waited with Parveen, I couldn't help but recall an interesting conversation I had had with a Muslim friend. She told me a plant is sometimes placed under the mother's bed during the delivery. It was, referred to as the "Mary Plant," named after the mother of Jesus. Muslims believe in the Virgin Birth and give reverence and honor to Mary. In fact, according to some accounts the town of Murree was named in honor of Mary. As for the "Mary Plant," local tradition held that the plant, not in bloom when first placed under the bed of a woman in labor, would be in full bloom by the time the baby arrived. I never found out the generic name for this plant.

I held Parveen's hand and rubbed her forehead with a damp cloth. The excitement grew as the head presented itself. After a few more pushes, the baby was born. A strong cry sounded and everyone was delighted at the birth of a healthy new baby.

In Muslim households, the first words a new baby hears are those of the Islamic creed: "There is no God but God, and Mohammad is the Prophet of God." Those in attendance then lift their hands in praise and thanksgiving and respond by saying, "*bismullah,*" in the name of God. Being a Christian family, we used the phrase "*Khudah ka shukar,*" thanks be to God.

The attendant reached for a butcher knife and cut the umbilical cord. A woman standing nearby grabbed the baby, turned him upside down over a metal bucket filled with water, and washed him. The baby was then wrapped in a cloth and handed to the mother.

Outside, the men standing around were told about the successful delivery, welcoming the good news. During the 1950's, American men celebrated a new birth by handing out cigars. In Pakistan, the custom was to deliver sweets to friends and neighbors. When a male child is born, the celebration can continue until well into the night.

Our youngest, Nancy, was born in 1959, two years after Jonathan came into the world. Like Jonathan, she was born at Rockedge in Murree. We looked forward to our third child.

For Jonathan, I had decorated a borrowed carriage for his crib. I loved getting yards of thin material and with a little ingenuity creating a lovely bed. When I knew that another baby was on the way, I bought a wicker basket designed especially for an infant. It had no legs but rested on a table top. With a canopy overhead, we could even take it outside and the baby would be protected from the sun. I bought yards of thin muslin-like cloth and decorated the basket with ribbons.

We thought the baby might arrive on Jonathan's birthday. However, June 27 came and went. Dr. Bruce was on leave and Dr. Hamm who had assisted at Jonathan's birth had come up from the mission hospital in Sialkot to attend.

We waited and waited and I became anxious, knowing that time was running out and Dr. Hamm would soon have to return to his regular hospital responsibilities on the plains. I took long walks and continued to wait. When the contractions finally began, Hu went for

Dr. Hamm. He also asked Mary Pegors, a missionary nurse who lived nearby, to come to the house.

Beforehand, I had prepared for those would attend me by baking cinnamon rolls and preparing coffee. Dr. Hamm and Mary Pegors arrived and we waited. The cinnamon rolls were beginning to disappear and still nothing happened. Around ten in the evening, Dr. Hamm decided it was a false alarm. Hu took him home and Mary returned to her family in an apartment nearby. We went to bed and slept well all night.

Next morning, Dr. Hamm's small daughter Suzy went to school and told all her friends that her daddy had delivered a baby girl for the Addletons during the night. Everyone knew I was expecting and accepted her news as fact. Meanwhile, we decided to take a ride in the Land Rover, hoping it might help precipitate labor. Hu and I drove around the mountain and ended up at the school. Surprised faces greeted us everywhere—I was still very much pregnant and the baby had not yet been born.

The Fourth of July arrived and we hoped the new baby might decide to come on this auspicious day.

It didn't happen. I enjoyed the celebrations with friends and colleagues. By nine that evening contractions had begun and Mary recommended that we send for Dr. Hamm. He came, although I feared it might once again prove to be a false alarm.

Nancy Elizabeth was born at five the next morning, her dark brown eyes wide open. Mary Pegors had been on duty for hours and we encouraged her to go home for some much needed rest and sleep. Another nurse, Anna Skrivanik, came around and looked after both of us. She insisted on staying the night, which turned out to be providential. Nancy produced a large amount of mucus and might have choked to death had not Anna been around to clear things up. We survived her birth and the boys were delighted with the safe arrival of their little sister. The gardener who had brought a bouquet of flowers on the occasion of Jonathan's birth remained out of sight when Nancy was born. Apparently, flowers were not considered for a baby girl.

Nancy was safe but all was not well in the country at large. Dr. Hamm had already extended his hospital leave by two weeks. It rained heavily across parts of Punjab during much of the time. Soon after

Nancy's birth, he returned to Sialkot. The town had been hard hit by heavy flooding. From the train station he had to take a boat to get to his home. On arrival, he discovered the water had flooded his house along with the rest of the hospital compound, reaching his bookshelves and destroying much of his library.

I felt terrible. He reassured us over and over that it was all right. From that time on, he referred to Nancy as his "flood baby."

Many years later, on Nancy's seventeenth birthday, all of us happened to be in Murree at the same time. Joining with another couple, we went out for a special dinner at the Golf Hotel, nestled on a mountainside in Bhurban. We couldn't help but note with astonishment how remarkable it was that Dr. Ham and his "flood baby" should be reunited after all these years.

—

Nancy turned yellow after her birth, just as Jonathan had turned yellow two years before. This time, a young doctor from New Zealand took care of her. However, I was not well. Dr. Coster checked on me as I began to bleed. It didn't seem serious to me and I was not especially worried.

Hu walked down the hill for a prayer meeting with some missionary colleagues. Jonathan and David were playing with a neighbor's children. A wide hallway separated us from our next door neighbors. They were home so I was not alone. I lay around reading and watching over Nancy. Suddenly, I felt warm blood and knew I was hemorrhaging. I did not panic. I simply whispered a prayer that God would take care of me.

I thought of going next door to seek assistance. However, Hu came home earlier than expected. Assessing the situation, he sent for the doctor. A D&C procedure had to be done. There were no operating facilities at the small clinic located further down the hillside. Hospitals were just too far away.

As often happens in small communities, word quickly spread among those living on the hillside that an emergency had occurred. Larry Johnson, a colleague who was gifted in every way, was able to make stirrups, creating the essential equipment. The doctor came, gave me light anesthesia and performed the procedure. Nancy and I spent the night at the clinic, looked after by a missionary nurse. We returned home the next morning.

About four years later, Nancy turned yellow again. She was not especially sick, but we knew jaundice is sometimes symptomatic of something more serious. Doctors confirmed she had a slight case of amoebic hepatitis.

"This is the second time Nancy has been yellow," I commented in an off-hand way to Ronnie Holland, a doctor as well as a close friend.

"And when was the first?" he asked.

I related to him the circumstances surrounding both her birth as well as that of Jonathan.

Dr. Holland immediately asked questions and became concerned enough to tell us quite frankly that we should postpone having other children until tests were run on me. He strongly suspected a blood incompatibility.

The next year when we were in the United States for home leave, we went through the required medicals. The doctor requested a Coombs test. When the results returned, my doctor couldn't wait to get in touch with me.

"This test shows the antibody count to be alarmingly high," he said. "I shudder to think what it was at the time of Nancy's birth." Both Hu and I have RH Negative blood type; I am type O and he is type A. However, there was an incompatibility between the sub-groups. Dr. Holland had told us to be thankful for three live, normal, and healthy children. We were now advised to have no more.

My Macon doctor suggested a tubal ligation. At the time, approval from a panel of doctors was required for this procedure. They had to determine if such a procedure was necessary for the health of the mother. My doctor assured me there would be no problem. We decided to postpone the procedure until we returned to Pakistan.

Soon after returning, I checked myself into a mission hospital. A highly-trained Pakistani woman doctor took care of me. Another national family planning campaign was underway, urging Pakistani families to have fewer children. Once again, incentives in the form of a few rupees or a radio were being offered. I suppose I could have asked for one or the other of these items. I wasn't interested. In this case, it was the hospital that received the remuneration - about two and a half dollars worth of rupees, which at that time was the financial incentive provided to Pakistani families when they made the decision to stop having more children.

Chapter Nine

CELEBRATING CHRISTMAS

It was Christmas Eve 1956 and we lived in Ratodero, ten thousand miles from home. For us, Christmas was always a special occasion spent with family and friends and marked by gifts, church choirs and nativity pageants. We were just three: our son David, who would soon celebrate his second birthday, Hu and me.

Situated on the edge of a desert in Upper Sindh, Ratodero perhaps most resembled Bethlehem some two thousand years ago. Most of the houses were made of mud or sun-dried brick. Camels, donkeys and oxen dotted the landscape. Not far away, shepherds watched their flocks of sheep and goats. The clear night sky in winter was magnificent with bright stars dotting the heavens and the Milky Way shining brilliantly through the dark. We were in the middle of nowhere.

Our own family Christmas was illuminated by one very dim electric light bulb hanging from the high ceiling of our living room. The windows were barred. Heavy wooden shutters closed off the view from outside. We had found a scrawny desert bush, tied it together with wire and string and put it in a pot of soil to hold it in place. A few homemade multi-colored paper chains decorated the tree. We were quite proud of the decorated tree we had managed to put together using local materials for our first Christmas in Pakistan.

Hu and I sat there, each of us alone with our own thoughts, remembering the loud, happy Christmases of years past. Polly and Ralph Brown and their children lived across town, celebrating their

136

Christmas Eve. There were no local Christians in this small out-of-the-way little town to share the holiday with us. Later, we would join colleagues for a time of celebration and sharing in a larger town some miles away. But, for now, it was just the two of us and our thoughts.

We had placed a few presents under our desert bush, lovingly wrapped and labeled. Suddenly and without warning, we heard a ticking sound coming from the small pile of gifts. I looked at Hu and he looked at me. Puzzled, I could not figure out what he was thinking.

Reaching for the gift that was ticking away, Hu burst out laughing and handed it to me.

I opened the package. It turned out to be a lovely but ordinary alarm clock, imported from England. I was overjoyed. We had forgotten to include a clock with us in our baggage. Hu had managed to find one in the local bazaar. His first Christmas gift to me in Pakistan would serve us well for many years to come.

———

On Christmas morning we joined the Brown family and journeyed to Larkana, a town where there was a church and a community of Pakistani Christians. We enjoyed a worship service that included carols, scripture reading, and a sermon in Urdu. It was meaningful to worship with local Christians on this special day, celebrated in diverse ways around the world.

Following the service, we mingled among the congregation and enjoyed tea and sweets before returning to Ratodero for Christmas dinner with our colleagues, Ralph and Polly Brown and their two boys. The spread that followed was magnificent, especially considering where we lived and the limited resources around us. The Browns had found a goose, fattened it up and cooked it to perfection, a fitting centerpiece for the table. We also had fresh vegetables, sweet English peas, mashed potatoes, creamed onions, stuffing for the goose and desserts. Polly prepared her favorites and I prepared mine. I managed to bake a carrot pie, my substitute for sweet potatoes. Between us, I think we must have had eight or nine desserts.

Dinner concluded with a Christmas fruit cake made with dried fruits and nuts from the local bazaar. Sugar was rationed. We went to the mayor of the town and requested a special allowance because of Christmas. He gladly signed off on the required paperwork and granted us the extra rations.

Very possibly, this first Christmas in Ratodero was the quietest one we ever celebrated in Pakistan. But the others, too, were memorable and exciting, each in their own way.

—

During the four years we lived in Ratodero, our family grew from one child to three. Aunts, uncles, grandparents and churches in the United States forwarded small Christmas packages to us by mail. While these gifts were always special, we also enjoyed finding ways to include local items. We were always on the lookout for special ways to surprise the children.

In the weeks leading up to Christmas, we noticed little lambs wobbling along after their mothers in the villages outside town. Our children were ecstatic. Occasionally, we stopped and organized an impromptu petting zoo. The shepherds were cordial and enjoyed meeting us, especially the foreign children.

Inevitably, the time came when David, Jonathan, and Nancy begged us for a lamb as a pet. After repeated pleas from them, we decided to surprise them with a little lamb for Christmas. Secretly, Hu went out to a nearby village and purchased the lamb.

We turned the lamb over to Baroo, our watchman, to bottle feed and care for until Christmas morning. Although we sometimes heard a plaintive "baa, baa" coming from Baroo's quarters late at night, somehow we managed to keep it a complete surprise.

Waking up early Christmas morning, Hu and I hung a red ribbon with a tiny brass bell around the lamb's neck and brought it into the house. Tying the lamb to a chair, we ran upstairs to bring the children down for their great surprise. When we returned, the lamb, wearing a quizzical expression, was nibbling away at the small desert bush we used for our tree.

All of us were thrilled and enjoyed raising, cuddling, and petting the lamb. It became a healthy adult sheep and the envy of many in the neighborhood.

At the end of four years, it was time for us to depart for our home leave in the United States. We would be away for one year. We had to find a home for our pet. There were those who wanted to puchase it from us, but we could not sell it. In the end, we gifted it to Partab who had provided faithful service as our part-time sweeper for four years.

Partab worked very hard at several houses. His young wife died of meningitis. He had children and later married again. Legally, there is no caste system in Pakistan. A sweeper, usually a Hindu or Christian, is viewed as the lowest of the low within the social and economic hierarchy of the country. Yet, sweepers perform essential tasks, not only keeping the streets tidy but also cleaning the putrid open street drains and toilets.

Our children were more than happy to pass their sheep on to Partab when we left for America. As it happened, Partab's oldest son was married while we were away. It was our beloved Christmas lamb that provided the sumptuous wedding feast for the celebration.

—

We never thought that we would hear the sounds of jingle bells in our remote corner of Sindh. When we returned from our first furlough in the United States, we moved to a larger town called Shikarpur. Our mission opened a hospital for women and children in Shikarpur. Women arrived, day and night, from every village and town in the district and sometimes beyond. Often, they arrived by ox cart.

The hospital was staffed by committed and highly-trained doctors and nurses. They were all single women with tremendous dedication and a single purpose: to serve the women and children in the province of Sindh.

While the core staff stayed many years, the hospital also relied on short-term volunteers from the United States and elsewhere who wanted to minister as well as gain the experience of temporary work at a medical facility overseas. We enjoyed our close relationship with these women. During their free time, they often joined us for picnics on the canal, shopping trips to Sukkur or game nights that usually involved Scrabble. Occasionally when they had an entire day off, they spent it in our home, providing a change of scenery as well as an opportunity to get away from the stress and heavy demands of a busy hospital. Always, they were a part of our family Christmas.

One year was especially memorable. A couple of young women volunteers were working at the hospital and this was their first Christmas away from home. We invited them along with the other nurses and doctors for a Christmas celebration.

We told the doctors and nurses in advance that we would provide transportation for their short ride to our house. Unknown to them, we arranged for a local camel driver to come with his large flat-bed cart to get them. He covered the cart with carpets, small bamboo seats and cushions. He also decked out his camel with large brass bells. Even the camel, usually smelly and bearing a very haughty expression, seemed to know he was on a special mission.

Our guests were dressed in their special Christmas clothes, waiting to for us. Rather than the sound of a Land Rover, they heard the distant sound of camel bells, jingling with each step. Soon, the camel entered the hospital compound and, much to their surprise, they saw Hu and the kids on the camel cart, shouting their Christmas greetings.

—

One Christmas Eve our family was mistaken for a band of angels. We had moved to Shikarpur. Ralph and Polly Brown lived alone with their children in Ratodero, a much smaller town some twenty-five miles away. Ratodero is a lonely outpost, more like a village than a town. We had spent our first Pakistan Christmas in Ratodero with the Browns and knew just how lonely it could be.

Now, several years later, we were celebrating another Christmas, this one in Shikarpur with Larry and Connie Johnson and their boys. On the spur of the moment, we decided to surprise the Browns and drive, unannounced, to Ratodero. We all piled into a Land Rover and started our journey.

It took well over an hour to reach the outskirts of Ratodero, where we parked the car. The vehicle was much too large for the small, narrow streets. We also wanted to keep this a surprise. Motor vehicles were rare in Ratodero. The Browns might come out to investigate the sound of a motor, no matter who was driving it.

Quietly, our little group tiptoed through the streets and stood outside the Brown's courtyard door. Loudly, lustily and with great enthusiasm we sang "Joy to the World."

Meanwhile, Polly was upstairs on the roof, near tears as she reflected on how far they truly were from home and family. She had spent days baking cookies and cakes. She realized her little family was alone, and there would be no one else to share Christmas with them this year.

Suddenly she heard singing. Looking up into the night sky, she thought it was the voices of angels, just as on the birth of Christ so many years before.

Peering over the wall, she looked down toward the narrow street below and quickly realized it was, in fact, not angels, but missionary colleagues from Shikarpur who had arrived. Calling for Ralph and the children, she ran down the long flight of stairs, opened the big wooden door, and invited us in. We celebrated together with cocoa, hot tea, and Christmas cookies, turning this impromptu caroling into a most wonderful Christmas for all of us.

—

Another of our Christmases in Pakistan was marked by war. It was 1971 and civil war had broken out between the two parts of Pakistan, West Pakistan where we lived and East Pakistan bordering Burma and India a thousand miles to the east. West Pakistan had long dominated the political and economic life of the country, fueling resentment among the Bengalis to the east. Soldiers from West Pakistan had been posted in East Pakistan to keep law and order. As the civil war continued, India increasingly became involved.

Our children were attending boarding school in Murree, more than seven hundred miles to the north. As India and Pakistan seemed to be moving toward open war, word came from the school that it was closing early and our children would be sent home with escorts by train. We were not given a time or date for their arrival. Because of the pending war, train schedules were uncertain and subject to change. For several days we waited anxiously until they finally arrived, dishevled and dirty from the long delayed train ride. The train track had passed within a few miles of the Indian border. Just a few days later, India and Pakistan were at war with each other and railway tracks and stations were being bombed up and down the country, including the train station at Rohri where our children had arrived.

For our children, the December 1971 war that pitted India against Pakistan and led to the birth of Bangladesh was an occasion for excitement, not fear. This excitement was fueled by occasional air raid sirens, warning that enemy planes were in the vicinity. A policeman was posted outside our front door. We were ordered to black-out all windows and told to remain inside. On occasion, the boys ventured up to the flat roof in the dark, checking to see if enemy warplanes were approaching.

Over the years, we had grown accustomed to living with uncertainty and political crises of various types. We lived through a number of coups and periods of civil unrest. We even maintained an evacuation kit including passports and other travel documents as well as a toothbrush, toothpaste, a changing of socks and underwear and other essential items.

The outbreak of war presented a serious crisis, especially when it quickly became clear that Pakistan would be on the losing side. We made plans for a possible evacuation by road through Afghanistan. Meanwhile, American officials at the consulate in Karachi were already making plans to evacuate their families by air. The Karachi harbor in particular was heavily bombed. There were also reports of the Indian army advancing on several provincial towns in Sind. Throughout the crisis, we maintained daily contact with the American Consulate in Karachi.

Our next door neighbors were from East Pakistan, adding further drama to the situation. In fact, Farid (not his real name) was the highest government official in our town, a member of the elite civil service dominating the local administration. A posting in Shikarpur was not highly prized but it was a step upward in the bureaucracy. Many of the sub-divisional magistrates, as they were called, serving in Shikarpur were young, highly educated and interesting.

Farid was newly married and arrived with his wife Hassina (not her real name), who was also from East Pakistan. Her father was vice-chancellor of a leading university in Dacca, East Pakistan's capital. As Bengalis living in a remote part of West Pakistan, their loyalties were bound to be questioned. For their part, they felt vulnerable living in a strange part of the country and far from home. Of course, they were also worried about their families in Dacca as the fighting there grew more and more intense.

Every evening when the black-out began, Hassina and Farid made their way to our house, sometimes climbing over the wall so as not to be seen. We listened attentively to the BBC for our news. Hassina was extremely anxious for news about her father, since it was reported that several dozen leading Bengali intellectuals had been taken out and shot.

With the children home, we tried to restore a sense of normalcy and even light-heartedness. We popped corn, decorated a tree and played table games.

The possibility of evacuation came up. Both Farid and Hassina were afraid we would leave and they would be left alone. We assured them of our help, even if we had to smuggle them out. Discussing how we could manage to do that, I had a wig and tried it on Hassina, effecting a marked change in her very classic and beautiful Bengali face. She laughed until she cried.

The days leading up to Christmas were quite subdued that year. Nevertheless, we celebrated with our dear neighbors and raised our hearts and voices in thanksgiving when the war was over. East Pakistan emerged as the new nation of Bangladesh while West Pakistan was now referred to as simply Pakistan. It was some time before the horrors and violence of the war became more widely known, at least among the Pakistani public.

What happened to our neighbors? Farid kept his job title but was transferred to another town. Before they left Shikarpur, they took the opportunity to give us many of their valuable items-rupees, jewelry, and clothes These had been all Hassina's wedding gifts. They left with us the names and addresses of their relatives in Dacca and Canada. We looked for every opportunity to return these treasures to their family, piece at a time. They were emphatic in telling us to throw everything away if we were ever compromised.

"Drop it in the Indus," Hassina said. "Destroy it; do anything but don't give it to the Pakistan Army."

It took some time, but in the end we successfully returned everything that had been entrusted to us. We enlisted help from friends who were traveling abroad. They took pieces with them to Dacca or gave items to others traveling to Bangladesh.

Much later, we learned of the trauma the young couple had to endure before finally returning to Bangladesh. For a time, they were detained at a camp for Bengalis set up in Karachi. From there, they were able to buy their freedom. They dressed as nomads. Hassina sewed rupees into the full skirt she wore. She sold her gold bangles, the only jewelry she had kept. The proceeds were used to transport both of them, first by train to Quetta and then on a truck loaded with goods going to Afghanistan.

Hassina and Farid were dropped off in the "no man's land" separating the two countries. Walking miles, tired, hungry, thirsty and afraid, they smuggled themselves into Afghanistan. They arrived weary, half sick, and nearly penniless. Ultimately upon reaching Kabul, they got a plane to New Dehi in India and then to Dacca and the waiting arms of their loved ones.

Hassina's father wrote us a letter of deep appreciation for the friendship we had given to his daughter and her husband. He told us that they had received the jewelry and other valuables and he would be forever grateful for the risks we had taken.

Some years later, we visited Dacca and arranged to meet them. Their experiences had aged them considerably. By this time, they had children and Farid had an important post in the government. We have since lost contact with them. We keep the memories tucked away and often they slip into our thoughts, especially during the Christmas season.

—

David graduated from high school in Murree in June 1973 and left for college in the United States. This was our first Christmas to be separated as a family. Thinking ahead, we planned a different kind of celebration.

We decided to spend Christmas away from home. Our mission maintained a small beach hut on the Arabian Sea at Hawkes Bay, just outside Karachi, for families to spend time together, away from the pressures of work. Every winter we spent a week at the "C-Breeze," as the beach hut was known. It was quite primitive with no electricity or running water. We had to bring drinking water with us. Each day, a camel driver brought jerry tins filled with water for bathing and cleaning up. Eventually, we managed to install a flush toilet. Over time, the inside furnishings and amenities were improved. It was a marvelous place to spend family vacations.

We hoarded imported items such as canned bacon and ham for our annual beach vacation. Before leaving home, I spent hours baking brownies, cinnamon rolls, cookies and anything that would keep without refrigeration. The evenings were spent popping corn or stirring up a batch of fudge. We played Rook, Scrabble, and other board games. Reading was also a favorite pastime.

Nearby villagers decorated their camels and horses, parading them up and down the beach and offering rides to children. Dusk was a special time as the sun dipped below the hills of the Kirthar range straddling Sindh and Baluchistan to the west. Looking out to sea, we could see the twinkling lights of the ships waiting patiently to dock at Karachi harbor.

During the morning we watched for dolphins. Often they obliged us, swimming up and down and around us in the water. The waves were good for riding. We watched the tide come and go, searching for shells or anything else washed ashore. Only a few steps on the sand separated our beach hut from the ocean.

If we were lucky, we saw giant sea turtles laying their eggs along the shore at night. Taking our Coleman lantern as well as a flashlight or two and searching up and down the beach, we looked for fresh turtle tracks. When we found them, we turned the lantern down low, turned off the flashlights and followed the tracks.

When we discovered a turtle in the process of actually laying eggs, we knew she would never leave until her task was complete. We sprawled out on the sand, inching close enough to see while also giving the turtle privacy as she lay over the hole she had dug with her flappers and, one by one, dropped her eggs. Once, we counted more than ninety eggs. As she labored, we noticed salty tears dropping gently from her eyes.

When the turtle finished, she quickly covered the hole with sand, turned around and went back to sea. The following year, she would return to lay eggs again on the beach where she herself was born.

While the turtles displayed incredible maternal instincts, they did not always get it right. On occasion, one would lose her sense of direction and head inland rather than toward the ocean. If we came across such a turtle and using all the might we could muster, we literally turned the 200 pound creature around and pushed her back to the sea. Once the turtle smelled the salt air, she took off on her own and left us.

At other times, as we walked up and down the beach during the day, we found turtles hatching. The small grey creatures pushed up from their womb of sand, one after the other, just as the eggs had been dropped some weeks before. Only a small number of the several dozen baby turtles hatched would make it to the ocean alive.

Both the eggs and baby turtles had predators. Mongrel dogs came along the beach at night, searching for food. They kept watch for the turtles, digging up the eggs and eating them as soon as the mother turtle left and returned to the ocean. It was not at all unusual to see broken turtle egg shells lying along the beach.

When finally hatched, the baby turtles raised their little heads, smelled the ocean and took off. Unfortunately, the mongrel dogs were often waiting for them, turning them into yet another meal. Even those baby turtles that finally made it to the water were sometimes snatched up by the large sea birds flapping about the beach.

David once provided some perspective when he suggested that we were simply witnessing the balance of nature at work. From another perspective though, the arrival of humans and mongrel dogs was providing an imbalance in nature and threatened these great sea turtles traveling from Karachi to the farthest reaches of the Indian Ocean. Fortunately, conservation efforts have been launched in more recent years along the Karachi coast in an effort to save these giant sea turtles from extinction.

On this particular Christmas vacation at the beach, we thought about David at every turn. Everything we did reminded us of our past times together. We bought a small potted evergreen plant for a Christmas tree and decorated it with small ornaments we had brought with us. I also opened a can of bacon and set out homemade cinnamon rolls, hot coffee, fruit and juice on Christmas morning.

For dinner, we decided to drive into Karachi to a restaurant featuring a special Christmas menu. December 25 is also the birthday of the Quaid-i-Azam Mohammed Ali Jinnah, the founder and chief architect of Pakistan. In his honor, the city was lavishly decorated with colored lights. Every mosque, official building and hotel glowed with illuminations of one kind or another. The five star hotels also lavishly decorated Christmas trees. In spite of the warm and balmy weather, it looked very much like Christmas.

We found a little restaurant called Maxim's on a quiet street in Clifton and sat down to an elegant dinner, starting with pink grapefruit sections dotted with pomegranate seeds. This was followed by a shrimp cocktail along with an entrée that included baked turkey, potatoes, fresh vegetables, cranberry sauce and hot rolls and butter. On top of everyting else, dinner ended with a flaming English plum pudding.

By the time we returned to our beach hut on Hawkes Bay, it was late and very dark. We missed David. Although away from home, there were reminders of him on every turn. We hoped he was enjoying his celebrations with family and friends. This was David's first Christmas away from home and our first without him-another deposit in our memory bank.

———

Scars on my right hand remind me of yet another Christmas in Pakistan. This one was in Hyderabad in 1974. Dr. Bruce had come from Shikarpur to spend the holiday with us. A relatively large community of missionaries lived in Hyderabad and we were hosting them for a carol sing and light refreshments.

I was in a hurry, working quickly to get everything ready for the special event. Dinner was planned early in order to have the kitchen tidy before guests arrived. The fish I wanted to serve was frozen and I needed it thawed in a hurry. After taking it from the freezer and letting it sit for awhile, it was still frozen. I grabbed a large butcher knife that had recently been sharpened and began to separate the pieces frozen together.

I am not sure what happened next. What I did see was blood flowing from my hand. Grabbing dish cloths to wrap around my hand, I ran to the hall yelling. I had been badly cut. Both Dr. Bruce and Hu came running. I sat on the floor crying, not from pain but from disgust at having hurt myself in this incredibly stupid accident.

Dr. Bruce wrapped my hand and set off to the bazaar with Hu. Before long, they returned with the needed supplies and she stitched three of the cut fingers on my hand. On one, the bone was showing. She gave me a mild pain killer and I begged her to put flesh colored band-aids on instead of a bandage until after the party. I also extracted promises from both Dr. Bruce and Hu to tell no one about the accident.

Our friends and colleagues arrived for the Christmas party. No one mentioned the bandages on my fingers. Because of the throbbing pain, I was constantly reminded of what had happened.

While enjoying refreshments, one little girl named Sarah Stock came and sat on my lap.

"Auntie," she said. "What happened to your fingers?"

"Shhhh," I whispered. "I did a very silly thing. I picked up a sharp knife and cut them. Don't tell anyone."

As far as I know, only the four of us knew about the accident. Sarah never said a word to anyone.

As a child, Sarah absorbed everything around her. She was also the first among my friends to discover that I had pierced my ears. I waited a long time to get this done. Traditionally, women in Pakistan have their ears pierced as infants. I had been in Pakistan for many years before I decided to pierce my ears. I asked Dr. Bruce to do the piercing for me.

Hu and I had to travel to Shikarpur for a business trip. I arranged for Dr. Bruce to pierce my ears while we were there. I should have brought small gold posts to go into the holes as soon as my ears were pierced, but I hadn't found the time to shop for them before the trip. Dr. Bruce simply put sterilized string into the holes and told me how to care for them. The string was not very obvious. In any case, my hair more or less covered my ears.

I was vain and did not want anyone to notice until I had new gold earrings dangling from my ears. Early on the morning we returned both the watchman and his wife were at the gate to welcome us. Immediately after our greetings and before we were barely inside the courtyard, the watchman's wife turned to me and said, "*Memsahib*, why didn't you tell me you wanted your ears pierced? I could have done it for you."

A couple of days later, Sara came for a visit. She too came quickly to the point.

"Auntie," she said. "Your ears—you've had them pierced."

I had just gotten insight from two sources into an interesting cultural nuance: in Pakistan, women always look at the ears first.

———

For many years the local congregation in Shikarpur met on our large verandah. Mats were rolled out on the hard tiled floor and we all sat with our legs crossed. Men sat in the front while the women and children sat in the back. *Purdah* is not a practice among Christians. Men and women do mix socially. However, a distinctly Pakistani decorum is observed. Women are modestly dressed, their heads always covered. They also remain reserved in their conversations with men. There is no touching.

Women found it difficult to walk through the streets in their Sunday clothes for church. Often they arrived with a load of small children on a horse-drawn *tonga*. This could be costly for families who already lived very meagerly, with little money available for extras. Yet, attendance at the weekly worship service was good, particularly on Christmas and Easter when the congregation included those from neighboring villages who sometimes arrived on foot or by oxcart.

Our courtyard was small but we always found room for everyone. After all, Christmas was the one big celebration of the year. In fact, the Christmas greeting in Urdu was *Burra Din Mubarak*, or "Blessings on the big day." Muslims all over Pakistan also used this phrase when offering greetings to Christian neighbors at Christmas.

Regardless of the time set for the service, people began arriving early, making themselves at home in our courtyard. Women and children came in their very best clothing. There was always an atmosphere of joy, even jubilation. The service lasted at least two hours or more. Carols were sung with enthusiasm. The Christmas story was retold, as had been done for centuries. With the final amen, members of the congregation turned and embraced each other with a genuine and heartfelt greeting.

Following worship, huge pots of steaming tea were served along with cookies and small cakes. We chatted and visited with each other until the setting sun signified it was time to return home. Hu and other colleagues packed their Land Rovers to capacity, providing transport to those who had no other way to get home. As they left, each child was given a piece of fruit or small gift to take with them to the village or *busti*.

—

Perhaps our most memorable Christmas in Shikarpur was the one when the local Christian community produced a live nativity. It rivaled those Biblical scenes in Cecil de Mille's movie productions.

The local Shikarpur Christian community, many of them eking out a living as despised sweepers on the fringes of society, loved the opportunity to celebrate. They also enjoyed hamming it up, responding instantly and appreciatively to the idea of producing a pageant in honor of the Christmas season.

Shikarpur with its palm trees, mud houses and dirt streets was an ideal setting for the Biblical drama. We provided very little advice and the local Christians did it all. In the end, everything seemed completely authentic, starting with the arrival of Mary riding in on a donkey and Joseph walking beside her. Baby Jesus was a small baby. The baby cooperated, sleeping placidly throughout the proceedings. Three wise men rode in on decorated camels, dressed like Eastern kings. Shepherds also arrived, bringing their sheep and goats with them.

The dim electric lights along with kerosene lanterns and the beautifully clear sky cast shadows across the scene of the crèche. The young men had practiced carols for weeks ahead of time. Now their voices were strong and resonant as they sang out Christmas hymns in both Urdu and Punjabi. Some were recognizable, having been translated from English. Others were indigenous and beautiful.

Members of the Christian community observing the pageant were joined by Muslim onlookers who had never seen such a production in our town. The creativity and enthusiasm displayed by this small minority, who lived and worked at lowly and sometimes demeaning jobs were both impressive and touching.

Later, our own three children, impressed by the pageantry of it all, insisted on producing their own performance for us at home, aided by bathrobes, silk scarves and other ordinary props.

At the end of the day, I was moved by the thought that on this day people throughout the world were re-enacting the birth of Jesus, whether in small family gatherings, churches large and small or great cathedrals. The two pageants I had just witnessed, first by Shikarpur's small Christian community and then by our children, were truly special, tenderly embodying what Christmas is all about.

Chapter Ten

EVERYONE LOVES A WEDDING

Customs and traditions surrounding weddings in Pakistan vary widely. Every one of the many dozens of weddings I attended was different, ranging from poor village weddings to sophisticated, expensive ceremonies hosted by the landed Sindhi aristocracy. The common theme throughout was celebration.

An engagement does not necessarily require an elaborate ceremony. However, it is always announced by the distribution of sweets among relatives and friends. Very often, the engagement has been in the making for a long time, in some cases, years. In fact, in some villages newborn boys and girls are pledged to each other by their parents at birth.

There is nothing new about an arranged marriage. Such a custom goes back to Old Testament times. Think of Isaac and Rebecca. It is not uncommon to marry first cousins. Marriage within the clan or caste is preferred. And marriage within a shared religious community is usually considered obligatory.

For instance, a Sunni typically marries a Sunni and a Shia marries a Shia. A Muslim woman is required to marry a Muslim. However, a Muslim man is allowed to marry a Christian or Jewish woman called "people of the Book." It is understood that children from the union will be raised as Muslim.

Pakistan's Christian and Hindu minorities also strive to ensure their sons and daughters marry within their faith. Sometimes Christian women, much to the displeasure of their families, marry outside their community.

—

Traditionally, the groom's family takes the initiative in negotiating an arranged marriage. The village barber has been known to play a role in bringing families together. After all, he knows all the men and boys in the area. Quite often in villages it is also the barber who circumcises male children. A wedding celebration itself is a useful venue for looking around for suitable matches. Astrologers are sometimes requested to provide guidance. Nowdays, advertisements in newspapers and on the internet bring couples together. As a boy nears adulthood, matrimony becomes an important topic of discussion within the family circle.

Women in the household have a vital role to play. After all, in a society where social segregation of the sexes is the rule, women know more about the eligibility of young women than anyone else. They can and do make recommendations.

Nothing is really ever said to the young man until the elders have reached consensus. After that, the young man is approached, usually by his father, and told of plans for his marriage to a specific girl.

A time is set for the prospective groom's family to visit the home of the prospective bride. This is an informal setting for the two families to meet. Pleasantries are exchanged over tea. Often the young woman is in an adjoining room, trying to listen in on the conversation. If she is lucky, she might even get a glimpse of the young man on this visit.

An arrangement is also made for the bride's family to visit with the family of the groom. Again, this is an informal time of getting acquainted. Both the young people are told that an engagement is in the offing. Technically, they can refuse. However, in all my years in Pakistan, I never came across a single instance in which children refused the decision about a marriage their parents had made.

The length of engagement varies from a few weeks to many months or even years. Usually, the preference is for a short engagement period. The agreement is binding, and, if the engagement is broken off by either side, it is considered a serious breach of protocol and results in deep embarrassment and humiliation.

The distribution of sweets to announce an engagement marks the start of a long series of joyous occasions. Women love a wedding and are in their element, making arrangements and shopping for clothes, jewelry, and household items. The groom's family selects clothes and jewelry for the bride-to-be. Likewise, the bride's family selects clothes for the groom. Arranging for food to feed the large number of people who will attend the festivities requires a lot of advance preparation.

—

I was elated and excited the first time I received a wedding invitation. I did not know the family well, but I enjoyed a circle of women friends who included me. They wanted me to share in the festivities because they knew I had never attended a local wedding.

My first concern was predictable enough: "What should I wear"?

Already, I had attended enough social teas to understand that my Pakistani friends dressed in beautiful clothes and jewelry for just about any social occasion. A wedding called for the finest.

I had decided soon after arriving in Pakistan I would wear the same clothes style as the locals, consisting of a *shalwar, kameez* and *dupatta*. The *shalwar* is a long full pants held up by a drawstring; the *khameez* is a loose-fitting tunic, reaching to the knees or below, and long or three quarter sleeves. The *dupatta* is a long diaphanous scarf that covers the head as well as the upper part of the body. These outfits are colorful, practical and very comfortable. They are ideal for the climate. For ordinary wear, I had outfits made from cotton and synthetic fabrics. Unfortunately, I did not have anything suitable for a grand wedding celebration.

With no ready-made clothing shops and not enough time to have an outfit made locally, I wore an American dress for my first wedding. It was one of the very rare times I attended a wedding wearing anything other than Pakistani clothes. Fortunately for me, western dress lengths were long during the 1950's. Besides, the social activities were segregated and men would not be around to gawk at me.

—

Hu and I went to the wedding together. The narrow street was adorned with multi-colored lights. The house itself was illuminated with hundreds, even thousands, of colored lights. A multi-colored tent was set up at one end, closing off the street. We could smell the aroma of spicy curries and kebabs as we walked toward the house where the wedding would take place.

When we reached the entrance, I was directed to the entrance for women and Hu left me and walked to the place where the men were. The women seemed pleased that I had come in my American clothes and admired the modest jewelry I wore. I quickly encountered a problem. Most women were seated, cross-legged on the carpet covered floor. The women must have immediately realized how impossible it was for me to join them on the floor. Instead, I was singled out to sit in a large, over-stuffed chair. At first I felt a bit chagrined. As the evening stretched out, I was more than pleased with my comfortable chair. I had been spared the indignity and embarrassment as well as the discomfort of trying to sit modestly in western attire, legs crossed on the floor.

Three or four other women sat alongside me on the large, over-stuffed chairs. Some of them spoke English, while I practiced my Sindhi. I wanted to ask a lot of questions.

My first question was, "Where is the bride"?

She was nowhere to be seen. In fact, few people had seen her for at least a week. I was told another ceremony had already taken place several days earlier, the first in a series of wedding events extended over a number of days. Close friends and relatives had been invited to that event.

I wanted to know about the ceremony I had missed. It had started with a recitation from the *Quran*. Afterwards, family and friends, all female, brought the bridegroom in for an initial celebration, complete with drums, musical instruments, and singing. At weddings I later attended, groups of transvestites, transsexuals or hermaphrodites dressed as women joined in the festivities. They were paid to participate and added color and excitement as they told risqué jokes, made fun of guests, sang and danced without inhibitions. They also performed for the men.

Throughout these rituals, the bride remained in her own room, dressed in ordinary clothes. Female relatives rubbed her with aromatherapy oils and ointments, ensuring a light, glowing countenance. Every day for a week, she would be anointed with these oils. She was not allowed to leave the room during this time, not even for a bath. She ate very little food. She always looked downcast and sad.

⸺

Another event had also taken place before the actual wedding. It was called the *mendhi* ceremony. *Mendhi* is the word used for henna, a traditional substance used throughout the Middle East and Asia as a hair coloring agent. In a Pakistani wedding, it is used to create a temporary tattoo on the hands and feet of the bride. Sometimes the groom's name is written and hidden in the bride's hands. On the night of the wedding, the bride will shyly ask her groom to look for his name in her hands.

As with almost every other wedding event, the *mendhi* ceremony is accompanied by singing and dancing. Sometimes it is spread over two nights. On the first evening, the women in the groom's household gather and put henna on the groom's hands. On the second evening, the ceremony moves to the bride's house. The guests sing and dance all night. Often the young girls perform a circular dance, holding lighted candles set in henna paste. Swinging the lighted candles rhythmically can be dangerous. At one such party I was fearful that Nancy's long dark hair might get singed.

The groom's female relatives and friends typically arrive at the bride's house for the *mendhi* as part of a large procession led by revelers playing musical instruments such as drums, trumpets and even bagpipes. The women arrive together, carrying a tray of *mendhi* as well as sweets to present to the bride and her family.

The procession is greeted warmly by the bride's family. Sometimes a friendly competition goes on between the groom's side and the bride's side to see who dances and sings the best. There is much laughter and all the guests participate. Everyone in the neighborhood knows a wedding is taking place because the laughter, music and drum beats go on well into the night.

The bride is conspicuous by her absence. However, she is very briefly ushered into the room to receive a blessing from various people. Her close friends and relatives escort her from her room into the room where festivities are taking place. Her *dupatta* is pulled down to hide her face. She is still in her days of seclusion and is not supposed to wear make-up or jewelry. Happily married women feed her sweets. Sweets assure a sweet married life. Several women may wave money over the bride's head, circling three times while doing it. Money wards off evil and gives blessings for a happy and prosperous life. The money is then collected and given to charity. When attending such events I tried to get into the feel of what was going on. I don't think I ever really understood it all.

——

The actual wedding day once again brings out a procession to the bride's home. As the groom leaves his house, a veil of flowers is placed over his face. He is presented with gifts and the family gives a blessing. Hired musicians as well as family members and friends dance joyously. Sometimes the groom sits on an elaborately decorated horse for his trip to the bride's house. If he travels by car, the car is festooned with flowers. This procession is called the *barat*.

Members of the bride's family stand outside their house to pass out garlands and welcome the procession. However, even now the groom does not meet his bride. Instead, he is taken to a large room or, more usually, a large tented area set up especially for male guests. Nervous and self-conscious, he is seated on a lavishly decorated chair. Guests line up to meet him, hanging garlands of flowers and money around his neck. This activity can go on for hours.

Meanwhile, the bride remains separate from the groom. After a long and luxurious bath, she is covered with more perfume and special lotions. Make-up is applied and her hair is styled. She just sits there, eyes downcast, while her friends transform her into a thing of beauty. Finally, her wedding ritual is about to begin.

The bride leaves the seclusion of her room. Arriving at the wedding venue where all the females have gathered, she is seated on the floor covered with beautiful carpets and surrounded by satin cushions. The careful attention and application of fragrance and oil during her secluded days is paying off—she positively glows. Her make-up and hair is perfectly done. Her red wedding dress is splendid and embroidered in gold. She wears heavy gold jewelry: rings on her fingers and toes, bracelets that nearly reach to her elbows, chandelier-like earrings that sparkle, a necklace around her neck and a beautiful jeweled ornament on her forehead, anchored by a gold chain attached to her hair.

All the while she is downcast, refusing to show even a trace of a smile. Her hands are folded demurely on her lap. Nearby someone softly fans her, using an ornate fan made especially for the occasion. Friends crowd around, blocking off fresh air. Finally, the groom is brought in to join the bride in the female section.

Both the bride and groom are represented by a family member. An attending religious leader is present and asks each of them, three times, if they approve the marriage. Always the answer is in the affirmative. The marriage documents are signed and the legal part of the wedding is officially over.

At the conclusion of these legal formalities, nuts and sweets are distributed to all guests. Sometimes gun shots are fired into the air. Applause goes up, both in the male domain as well as in the secluded female domain.

Dinner is served, complete with mounds of rice trimmed in thin silver paper, bowls of lamb curry, and hot breads. The men are served first, followed by the women and children. Guests stand around holding their plates in their left hand and eating with their right hand. The task of eating with one's fingers is an art, one I confess I never completely mastered.

Food is a highlight of any wedding and is invariably delicious. At one wedding, I was told that no one remembers what really happens at a wedding, not even the bride and groom-the only unforgettable part is the food.

Guests begin to depart as soon as dinner is eaten. The crowd dwindles until only family members are left.

It is now time for the couple to meet each other. The two sit together on a carpet-covered floor, separated only by a large satin cushion. Both are veiled. A mirror is brought and placed on the cushion. A large scarf is spread over both of them. Slightly lifting their veils, they glance into the mirror and finally look into each other's eyes for the first time.

Someone waves a *Quran* over their heads and recites a blessing. The bride and groom are then given a glass of almond milk, both drinking from the same glass. They feed each other sweets.

Introducing some fun into the solemn occasion, happily married women are encouraged to knock the heads of the couple together. Taking turns, they also whisper marriage advice to the couple. I participated in this ritual once at the wedding of a young friend. While knocking their heads together, I whispered advice as well as a little humor. The bride actually gave me a smile. Meanwhile, the bride's sisters steal one of the groom's shoes and hold it for ransom. Friendly negotiations continue amidst laughter until the two sides agree to a redeeming price.

Following these lighter moments, the most poignant ceremony of the entire week takes place. It is time for the bride to leave with her groom. Legally, they are now married. The father of the bride and her brothers come to give her away. She will now join her husband in the house of his father. Women from the bride's family cry, sometimes even wail. The bride, still downcast, sheds tears. She has known only the love of her father's house for her entire life. She is leaving this cocoon of love and security for a household she has never known.

Bravely, she hugs her family and joins her husband in this somber leave taking. A married female family member accompanies her to her new home for a few days. Later the groom's family hosts another dinner, this time for the couple who are now husband and wife. The dinner, called *Valima*, signals the marriage has been consummated and their life together has begun. A week or so later, the bride goes back to her home for a short visit.

—

There were a million questions I wanted to ask at that first wedding. What I learned helped me to understand the hundreds of others I attended. I'm still learning because modern innovations continually influence ancient customs and traditions. Nowdays, large commercial wedding halls and hotels are often the venue for weddings. Videos and digital cameras have become essential. Honeymoons, often taken in the Murree hills, are gaining popularity. I'm glad I was there before these modern changes began.

Over the years, I accepted nearly every invitation that came my way. I must admit sometimes the long hours of waiting for something to happen could grow tiresome and even boring. However, it was during those hours that I asked questions from among the women around me. As I found out, although no two answers are always the same, they are similar enough to know that weddings are special events and everyone loves a wedding.

——

Both of us were invited to a Muslim wedding in the Punjab province, quite a distance to the north from where we lived. We had met the young man while he served as a magistrate in Shikarpur. He was a member of the elite civil service. Not only was he handsome, he was university educated and western in his outlook. He had recently become headman of his village. In spite of western influence, he followed the tradition and custom of an arranged marriage.

Attending the wedding presented a language challenge. Our language was Sindhi and his village people spoke Punjabi. Urdu is the national language and Hu was fluent in that language. I understood Urdu but was self-conscious and lacked confidence in speaking it. I memorized a phrase in Urdu that always served to put me in good grace with my hosts. Translated loosely, it meant "I can understand Urdu but in speaking, I have no power."

The minute we arrived on the premise, Hu was escorted to the large area reserved for men and I was taken to the women's section. I knew absolutely none of the women. Around me they were all speaking Punjabi. I gulped, pulled my *dupatta* around me, and smiled.

An elderly woman came to my rescue. She assigned a young college woman who spoke English to hang out with me. She stayed with me, helped me when I tried to speak Urdu and introduced me to various family members.

Large tents had been set up to accommodate hundreds of guests. Nearby, huge cooking vessels over open fires simmered with chicken curry and rice. Several men squatted near clay ovens, baking *naan*, delicious bread. Little girls and boys dressed in colorful outfits danced happily about. Women laughed and chatted with each other throughout the night. All of them wore expensive outfits and gold jewelry set with rubies, emeralds, and diamonds. I'm not sure where the music was coming from, but local musicians kept us entertained the entire time. Young women performed classical and folk dances.

At one point, I was taken to a large room filled with wedding gifts–quilts, bed spreads, sheets and pillow cases, table linens, electrical appliances, china sets, tea sets, cutlery, cooking vessels, clothes, jewelry, furniture, carpets and on and on. Stacked to the ceiling, the couple had received in multiple numbers, a storehouse of personal and household goods. The villagers indulged their chief on his wedding day with such an array of gifts.

I missed the actual marriage ceremony. It took place before we arrived. However, I was invited to meet the bride. Describing her as beautiful is an under-statement. She looked like a Mughal portrait or someone from out of *Arabian Nights*. Her dark hair, magnificently arranged, shone with tiny specks of gold dust. Her make-up was flawless and eye shadow had also been dusted with gold. Jewels sparkled on her forehead, arms, fingers, toes and in her ears. Her wedding attire was different from others I had seen. Although it was red and elaborately embroidered with pearls, gold thread and glass beads, she wore a very full pants skirt. It reminded me of palazzo pants. Over the skirt was a fitted bodice, also adorned with jewels and embroidery. Her *duputta* was imported chiffon with matching embroidery, gold thread and pearls. The complete outfit must have weighed heavily on her slim body. For this day, at least, she was a queen.

Double weddings sometimes happen and on occasion we were invited to attend. Two sisters were marrying two brothers. These young people were Christians. The young men were from Quetta while the young girls lived in our community. They belonged to the sweeper class and lived in a *bustie*. The brides were semi-literate and the grooms were literate and employed. Economically, both sides were equally matched; not wealthy by any means, yet not destitute.

Everyone was pleased with the creative match-making that led to the arrangement. A double wedding was also very economical. Given the distances involved, the families had only to bear the expenses of one long journey rather than two, and the wedding feast for two couples cut expenses even more.

The wedding took place in the middle of the morning. A Catholic priest and a Protestant clergyman performed the ceremony. Unlike traditional Muslim weddings, there was no segregation of the sexes. All the guests were accommodated under a single large and colorful tent set up to provide shade. However, men gravitated in groups and the women sat together. We all sat on woven carpets or straw mats.

Pre-wedding ceremonies largely followed the pattern I had seen at Muslim weddings. The two grooms arrived with their friends and relatives by train. Hired local musicians accompanied the procession as it made its way to the wedding tent.

We watched with interest as the wedding party arrived. Activity was going on all around us. Barking dogs, clucking hens, and crying babies were a normal part of life in the Christian *bustie* and a wedding ceremony was no different. It, too, had to fit in with whatever else was going on.

The Catholic priest arrived first on a motorcycle, followed by the Protestant minister. With their arrival, the guests quieted down and the ceremony got underway.

The two brides walked down a short aisle, looking beautiful in their traditional red outfits, modest array of jewelry, and hands and feet covered with intricate henna designs.

The priest and minister read, in turn, from a prayer book and each couple, recited their vows. The service was conducted in Urdu.

Following the ceremony, congratulations were happily given to the couples and their parents. A special rice dish, *biryiani* was served to the guests.

The celebration had been purposefully arranged so the wedding party could depart by train for Quetta in the evening. The departure was a bittersweet moment. A strange new environment awaited the young brides, vastly different from the one they had known growing up in Shikarpur. In this case, the two brides were sisters and could share in the transition together.

Even so, leaving home was not easy. In spite of tears, there was also laughter and joy. Once again, the musicians joined in leading the procession to the train station. Big bundles containing clothes and household goods were loaded on the train. The conductor blew his whistle and the train pulled out of the station, taking two young brides to their new home.

—

Until partition, a large Hindu population lived in what is now the Islamic Republic of Pakistan. While many fled to India following independence in 1948, some stayed behind, especially in the province of Sindh. Indeed, some of the Hindus where we lived had been very wealthy merchants and had to leave large houses and profitable businesses behind.

We always enjoyed meeting members of the remaining Hindu community scattered around various parts of Sindh. It was interesting to learn more of their family history, the reasons they stayed in Pakistan and the way in which they interacted with the majority Muslim population around them.

I was happy when the embossed invitation to attend a Hindu wedding arrived, providing an opportunity to learn about their customs and approaches to marriage. And, when it came time for the ceremony, different from a Muslim ceremony, I had a lot of questions.

Months before the wedding, the engagement had taken place with ceremony. The newly-engaged couple had been given jewelry and clothing by the respective families. Marriage is considered a sacrament within the Hindu culture, and three values are emphasized above all others: growth, harmony and happiness. An astrologer had been consulted to ensure perfect timing for the actual wedding ceremony.

The couple were led into the wedding hall and sat underneath a canopy, separated only by a curtain. It was lowered and the couple exchanged garlands, symbolizing acceptance and respect for one another.

Everything following was equally as rich in symbolism. For example, an elderly family member placed a white cotton cord around the couple's shoulder. This rite was meant to protect the new couple from evil while also signifying the eternal bond that had now developed between them. Holding hands, the couple vowed to love, cherish and protect each other. Taking the white cotton cord, the priest tied the wedding knot to indicate the permanency of their union.

The bride's father offered honey and yogurt to the groom. On some occasions, I was told, the father-in-law washes the right foot of the groom as an expression of respect. The bride's father placed his daughter's hand into the groom's hand, requesting him to accept his bride as an equal partner.

At this point, the priest stepped forward to light a sacred flame. The couple invoked the god of fire to witness their vows. The bride then placed her right foot on a stone, the groom admonishing her to be firm as a stone in the face of anything life might throw their way.

I watched with interest as the couple walked four times around the fire in a clockwise direction, each walk representing a religious or moral goal in life such as prosperity, earthly pleasures, or spiritual salvation.

Next, the pair took seven steps together around the fire, reflecting an old Hindu tradition that if two people take seven steps together they remain friends for life. Each step also involved a wedding vow; the first to honor and respect each other; the second to share joy and sorrow; the third to trust and to be loyal; the fourth to learn together, emphasizing the value of knowledge, values, sacrifice and service; the fifth to remain committed to purity, family duties and spiritual growth; the sixth to affirm the principles of righteousness; and finally, the seventh a promise to cultivate and nurture an eternal bond of friendship and love.

At the end of each walk, the bride opened her hands. Her brother filled her open hands with puffed rice, signifying prosperity and wealth. The parents of the bride and groom dipped a rose in water, sprinkling it over the couple and giving them their blessing. The couple touched each other's heart, making promises to each other. They fed each other. The groom applied a small dot of red pigment to the bride's forehead, welcoming her as his life's partner.

Previously, I had seen Hindu women wearing a red dot on their forehead and wondered why. During the marriage ceremony, this is done for the first time when the groom himself applies the pigment. Therefore, I was told, only married women wear this dot.

The parents blessed the couple again and the couple touched the feet of their parents, showing respect.

As in a Muslim ceremony, the hands and feet of the couple were decorated with henna, the names of the bride and groom hidden in the design. Friends at the wedding also told me the new bride is not expected to do any housework until the henna has faded away.

The formal ceremony concluded with a blessing from the priest. Guests were showered with rose petals and rice as friends and relatives lined up to meet the newlyweds to give them a personal blessing. The women dressed in *saris* rather than the traditional *shalwar, kameez, duputta* most often seen in Pakistan. The bride's *sari* was red and elaborately embroidered in gold thread. Laden with gold necklaces, bracelets, and rings, she sparkled. As in Christian weddings, men and women mixed more freely than in the Muslim ones I had attended.

—

Parsees are yet another religious minority in Pakistan. Numbering only a few thousand, they live primarily in Karachi. Their already small numbers are diminishing not only in Pakistan but also around the world because of a continuing trend toward smaller families and a religious culture that frowns on conversions. The Parsees in South Asia had first come as merchants and then refugees from Persia, where they had practiced the ancient Zoroastrian religion until the rise of Islam. After fleeing Persia, many Parsees settled in the area in and around Bombay.

My first encounter with a Parsee had been on a ship going from England to Bombay, India in 1961. We traveled together up to Karachi, the last port of call before reaching Bombay. A Parsee gentleman on board became friendly and we exchanged many pleasant conversations.

One interesting fact he shared on board the ship was his community's belief the wise men that came from the East at the birth of Jesus were Zoroastrians. Later, I heard the same thing from other Parsee friends in Pakistan.

Often, when we traveled on passenger ships between the United States and Pakistan, Hu was asked to lead a worship service on Sunday. I was surprised to see our Parsee friend in attendance. He sat alone, just in front of me. After the service, we chatted a while. He said he especially enjoyed the hymns and told me that he had never heard such beautiful singing. Our religious differences did not detract from our social encounters at all. We met several times throughout the voyage.

The next time I met a Parsee was in Pakistan. He was a young business man who assisted us with some legal matters. He was handsome and a bachelor. There was a Parsee temple in Karachi and we passed by it now and then. It was easy to single out Parsee women on the streets because of their dress. Usually, they wore western clothes and always seemed well-dressed and attractive.

Some Parsees were well known for their philanthropy. Despite their very small numbers, prominent Parsees in Pakistan have included a leading hotel magnate, the owner of the country's only functioning brewery and Bapsi Sidhwa, a novelist who writes in English and has since migrated to America. We enjoyed our several encounters with the Parsee business man and, in due course, received a beautiful invitation to his wedding.

The wedding was held in a large hotel and involved several hundred guests. The main ceremony took place on a stage set above the audience. The groom arrived first, dressed in white. He carried a shawl in his hand, symbolizing respect and greatness. A long mark was on his forehead.

The bride followed. She was dressed in a gorgeous white *sari*, heavily embroidered. In contrast to the elongated mark on the groom's forehead, she had a rounded red mark. His mark, I was told, signified a ray of sun while hers symbolized the moon. These marks were meant to show the nature of the relationship: the sun emits rays which are absorbed and reflected, allowing the moon to shine.

Trays of rice had been placed on tables beside the couple. According to one guest, the rice symbolized prosperity. However, another guest told me that the rice was there to indicate fertility.

A small metal pot containing clarified butter and molasses was also placed on one of the tables. The butter, soft and runny, indicated gentleness and courtesy while the molasses served was symbolic of sweetness and a good disposition. Meanwhile, two candles burned nearby while a servant waved two censers; one contained frankincense and the other fire to suggest purity as well as plenty.

The couple remained separated by a curtain as two Parsee priests walked around the chairs, enclosing them in a circle. The ends of the cloth were then tied together. In effect, the priests were literally tying the "marriage knot." When the bride and groom finally joined hands, the curtain was dropped and the two, once separated, were now united by the bonds of matrimony.

The bride and groom joined right hands which a priest tied together in a "hand fastening ceremony." A string was wound around seven times. By itself, it could easily be broken. However, when twisted into a single strand, it was nearly impossible to tear apart; emphasizing this union could never be broken.

Close relatives served as official witnesses. One priest asked the groom if he were willing to take the woman to be his wife and a similar question was asked of the bride. Marriage, once embarked upon, is supposed to last a lifetime. The same question was asked two or three additional times, just to make sure. Each of the priests spoke to the couple, admonishing them on how to behave as husband and wife.

I was astonished when, at the end of the ceremony, the couple kissed in front of all the assembled guests. Ordinarily, such a public display of affection would never be seen in Pakistan. In fact, couples have been apprehended by the police for kissing or even hugging in public.

With the ceremony complete, the guests lined up to greet the newlyweds. A band struck up modern tunes and an enormous feast was served in the hotel garden. Fairy lights shone and twinkled in the early evening shadows as we all mingled about, talking to each other and wishing the new couple happiness in the years ahead.

Looking back, I can't help but think that weddings were one of the highlights of my many cultural encounters in Pakistan. Partly, it is because I was able to attend ceremonies reflecting the many religious communities in Pakistan–Muslim, Christian, Hindu and Parsee. Also, these weddings cut across the entire social strata of the country. Although there were certain common strands in all of them, there were important differences as well.

Over time, I also learned to expect the unexpected. In one very remote village wedding, we waited up all night for the wedding party from a neighboring village to arrive. It never did and eventually we had to leave. Later, I learned, the wedding did in fact take place, though a day later than originally planned.

Once I was asked to design the flowers for a large Christian wedding in a nearby city. Flowers were brought in from other cities, and I had a lot of fun making the bouquets. Many Christians have adopted western customs in some of their celebrations. Often, especially in middle and upper class families, the bride will wear a white gown and veil rather than the elaborate red outfit more properly called the "traditional" Pakistani bridal costume.

Another time, I was asked to bake a wedding cake. The baking part was easy, but cake decorating was beyond my area of expertise. I found a beautiful white silk flower from my own accessories and with narrow ribbon streamers managed to create an acceptable wedding cake of beauty.

On another occasion, I was asked to do the hair of a young Muslim friend who was getting married. Her hair was beautiful, very long and straight. I had a blow dryer and a curling iron. With help from her friends and a little gel, we managed to curl, swirl, and pin, giving her a presentable hair do for her wedding day. Her friends were skilled in applying make-up. She sat quietly while we all worked to make her special for her wedding day. Modern brides in Pakistan now have professionals who specialize in bridal make-up. Beauty salons are big business in most cities.

As an ordained minister, Hu was recognized by the Government of Pakistan as having the credentials to perform wedding ceremonies for Christians. He was called on to do this many times, both in the Pakistani Christian community as well as among the diplomatic and business community. Our home was used several times for expatriate weddings. I would rush around beforehand, cleaning the house, collecting flowers and bringing out the candles.

Once, Hu was asked to bring the homily at a wedding taking place at Holy Trinity Cathedral in Karachi. Built in 1855, it was the first Protestant church ever constructed in Sindh. The wedding involved a well known couple and many non-Christians attended. Afterward, we were surprised when a large number of the young couples who attended asked for a copy of his sermon. They liked what they heard regarding Christian teaching about marriage.

One of the biggest weddings that we attended while living in Karachi involved two people from Pakistan's small Chinese community. Years ago, a number of Chinese families migrated to what is now Pakistan and what was then part of the British Empire. Some were involved in trade and others opened restaurants or worked in various service occupations. Like the Parsees, the Chinese Pakistanis represent a small but important part of the complicated social mosaic that makes the country so interesting.

The bride operated a beauty salon out of her house and I went to her for my haircuts. She was popular in Karachi and her clients included women from both the expatriate and the Pakistani community. She was engaged to a Chinese doctor who practiced the ancient Chinese method of medicine. Both were older and had previously been married.

I had an appointment with Ms. Wu early one morning. Hu dropped me off and left for errands. As soon as I opened the gate, I was met by a huge Alsatian dog, snarling and baring his teeth at me. I let out a yell. Between my yelling and the dog's barking, Ms. Wu ran out and pulled the dog away from me. He had caught me in the seat of my jeans, ruining the only pair of designer jeans I ever owned.

Ms. Wu took me inside and made a cup of tea. She assured me that the dog had been properly vaccinated. She called her fiancé, the doctor, and asked him to send some Tiger Balm. Although I was upset, we went on with my appointment. As she cut my hair, she explained that someone had left the dog out and the person responsible would be reprimanded.

Hundreds of Pakistanis who have been bitten by dogs die from rabies each year. However, this was not my only concern. Tetanus is endemic and my doctor told me I should also get a tetanus booster shot, just to be sure I was covered. The fact that I am allergic to a tetanus vaccine made from horse serum complicated matters. When I told this to the hospital staff, they recommended a synthetic vaccine and also advised me to call my husband as he should be with me when I got the shot. I was apprehensive.

While waiting for Hu to arrive, I was ushered into a room with an attending doctor and nurse. A large canister of oxygen was rolled in and I was told to lie down on what looked like an operating table. I was injected and ordered to stay there for about an hour while my vital signs were monitored. All went well and there were no repercussions. When I got home that evening, I wondered what the Chinese doctor would have done.

Despite this problematic early encounter, the invitation to the Chinese wedding duly arrived. Attached to the invitation was a security check list providing information on what to expect when the chief guest, as yet unnamed, arrived. We arrived early, anticipating possible difficulty in accessing the wedding hall. The guest of honor–President Zia al Haq and his wife–came later, once all the guests had arrived.

The event turned out to be more a celebration dinner than an actual wedding. It was held in the huge ballroom of a five-star hotel. We were ushered to our seats, right on the front row. Local musicians and comedians kept us entertained. We visited with the guests on our left and on our right.

When the President and his entourage arrived later in the evening, they took their seats on a dais, bodyguards carefully watching from some distance behind. We were pleased to meet the President and his wife. Not many months later, President Zia al Haq was killed in a plane explosion in southern Punjab, along with the American Ambassador and the senior US military attaché in Pakistan.

Ms. Wu and her doctor husband were closely acquainted with the President. The President had learned of the doctor's medical prowess, especially in acupuncture. Mrs. Zia al Haq was in poor health and the doctor was often summoned to Islamabad to care for her. Ms. Wu also attended the First Lady for her beauty needs–and now the First Lady was showing respect and appreciation by attending her wedding.

—

Another wedding incident that occurred when we lived in Karachi also left a lasting memory. Sometimes, I wish I had not been there. It involved a large wedding celebration with many hundreds of guests. I had been to other elaborate and expensive weddings, but the glitter, jewelry and large number of dignitaries astounded me.

Earlier in the evening, we had arrived back in Karachi after a visit with a poor Christian family in the interior of the country. We had reminisced about a wedding in their family some years earlier. The contrast in my world that day could not have been clearer. I put myself, heart and soul, into both worlds. Indeed, it was one of the astonishing ironies of being a missionary in Pakistan–not being in a set class of our own, in a matter of hours we mixed with the richest and most powerful as well as the poorest outcast in the land.

The wedding was one of the biggest social events in Karachi that evening. We mingled with guests, some of whom we knew and others of whom we only read about in the newspapers. We talked briefly with Benazir Bhutto, then the Prime Minister of Pakistan. I had last seen her as a small child in Larkana back in the late 1950's when she had accompanied her mother Nusrat to a party hosted by my colleague Jean Buker. At that time, the little girl was known as "Pinkie."

Benazir was more beautiful in person than can be imagined. She had already experienced considerable tragedy in her young life. These tragedies included the hanging of her father by President Zia al Haq and the untimely death of her brothers who had become embroiled in various political controversies. Years later, she herself would be assassinated after returning from years of exile to run for re-election. On this occasion, she played the part of Pakistan's first female Prime Minister, moving freely among guests and engaging with each of them on a personal level. Our daughter Nancy and her husband Jeff, newly wed, were visiting us in Pakistan. They met Benazir at the wedding and she animatedly told Nancy that she vividly remembered her own wedding day. Benazir's marriage had been an arranged one.

The wedding ceremony had already taken place before we arrived and the bride and groom, dressed in usual splendor, were accepting greetings from the large crowd.

I met an old friend whom I had not seen in some time. She asked me if I had met the other family. I was not sure what she meant so I asked her. I was told that the bride's father had another family, a village family. They, too, were attending the wedding celebration. This second family observed *purdah* and was sitting in a screened off section of the wedding hall. None of them would venture into the crowd where males and females were standing, eating, and visiting together.

I followed my friend to the enclosure, and she introduced me to all of them. First, I met the wife and then the children. I hoped I did not show the astonishment I felt when I was introduced to a beautiful daughter, another daughter of the father of the bride. She was from her father's other wife, his village wife.

The young daughter resembled the bride in every way. She even appeared to be about the same age as the bride. However, there was a slight contrast. She was less fair in complexion than her step sister. They had the same father but different mothers. One of the mothers came from the village, the other from America.

At some level, the scene of two wives attending the same wedding ceremony as their shared husband seemed to capture the sometimes uneasy way in which even the wealthiest and most educated Pakistanis balance the demands of tradition with a wider and more rapidly changing world. In this case, the father did it by maintaining two families, one deeply conservative and living in the village, the other much more cosmopolitan and living in Karachi.

Reflecting on the wedding these many years later, it almost seems like a metaphor for the difficult balancing act faced by those seeking to simultaneously adhere to the conservative Islamic traditions of Pakistan while also remaining connected to a very different outlook on life. Even as a wealthy businessman, the father had a foot in both worlds and most probably both were equally important and meaningful to him. I had to wonder what his American wife felt about being one of two wives. I also wonder how the new bride deals with her step sisters or even tries to explain her personal situation to friends in America where she lives.

Tying the knot, feeding each other, lighting candles, veiling, exchanging vows, keeping relationships straight among various ex-wives, ex-husbands, step children and step siblings—at times, it all seemed complex and challenging. And yet, on further reflection, these customs aren't so strange when I analyze some of our own wedding traditions and the various ways in which they have evolved over the years.

Chapter Eleven

A SPECIAL VILLAGE

Our mission's ministry was diverse. The small minority of Pakistani Christians scattered around upper Sindh was one aspect. We helped in starting a small school for very poor Christian children who otherwise would not have had this opportunity. Training church leaders was important. Also, we were keenly interested in building bridges with the wider Muslim community that surrounded us. Building a hospital for women and children reached out to a large area. Patients came from long distances for expert medical care. For a number of years, Hu's work included a focus on Bible translation and publishing Christian literature.

Unexpectedly, we became involved with a rural community of tribal people we had previously known almost nothing about. They were *Marwari Bhils*. Ostensibly Hindu, they practiced an ancient tribal culture going back hundreds if not thousands of years. During the 1960's, Domji, a prominent Marwari leader in upper Sindh, became a Christian. After his conversion and baptism, he invited our family to visit his village.

Domji lived some seventy miles northeast of Shikarpur, on the other side of the Indus River near the small town of Ghotki. We packed a tent, portable kerosene stove, bedding, and food supplies for a week. These were very poor people and we did not want to burden them with our needs.

It seemed as if the entire village was waiting for us. David and Jonathan were in boarding school. Nancy, not yet in boarding, came with us. She was five years old and quickly became the center of attention.

The initial conversation between Hu and Domji dragged on for a long time. I could understand some of what they were saying. The longer it continued, the more apprehensive I became. When it ended, I was not at all surprised when Hu came over to me and said, "We will not be staying in our tent."

The Marwaris ranked near the bottom of Sindhi society. Upper class Sindhis, whether Muslim or Hindu, wanted nothing to do with them. As we later found out, Marwaris were routinely denied service at the tea shops along the roadside. For us as Christians, espousing equality for all, to reject the hospitality offered to us would be a grave insult. We would not only sleep with the Marwari villagers, we would eat their food and live with them.

This settled, we were shown to our hut. The dirt courtyard in front of the mud huts had been swept clean. The hut to which we were directed was also very clean. Furnishings were simple–two rope strung beds covered with a patchwork quilt and colorful comforters. There was no electricity.

Not long after we had settled in, the local women, squatting around an open fire, called us for tea. First, the men were served tea and bread and then Nancy and I were served ours. The conversation continued for some time. After a long while, we excused ourselves and returned to our hut. We were sleepy and already it was nearly midnight.

—

Before going to bed, I improvised an inside toilet for emergency use. We brought a small chamber pot with a cover, which we placed in a corner behind a make-shift privacy wall made from a blanket. There was no door in the hut, just an opening in the wall. A couple of windows were, likewise, holes in the wall. Nancy and I hopped in one bed, Hu in the other. We slept in the clothes we had worn all day, just as the villagers did.

Even in Sindh, it can get cold at night. Snuggling under the covers, Nancy and I tried to get warm. We wanted to settle down for the night. Suddenly I realized we were being watched. I closed my eyes, pretending to be asleep. I sensed movement in the room. A continuous stream of people passed in and out of our mud hut. As one person left, others came in. Their movement created eerie shadows. Later I told a friend I now know what it is like to lie in state.

After everyone's curiosity had been satisfied, the village became quiet and the fire outside died down. It was well past midnight. I couldn't sleep. Nancy couldn't sleep. I began to itch. Nancy itched and became more restless. I imagined the mosquitoes were eating us alive, bringing malaria with them. Or, perhaps, we were being bitten by fleas and soon come down with typhus fever. I felt something crawling on me. Cringing, I just knew it was a spider.

Suddenly, a loud sound interrupted my thoughts and I sat up in bed. A dog had entered the hut and knocked over an empty metal cooking vessel. Just outside the hut, a man began coughing and he continued to cough throughout most of the night. I heard him repeatedly clear his throat, spit and then cough again. Now, I worried about tuberculosis. I began to wonder: can I possibly endure the week ahead in this kind of environment, in this remote and isolated place?

Worry was consuming me. Mentally, I was trying to figure out a respectable way that Nancy and I could leave in the morning. Back and forth my thoughts wandered, and I became more agitated. Something had to give. Finally, I awoke Hu. Tearfully, I told him that I just could not stay for a week in this place. Besides, I was afraid Nancy might become sick. He understood my feelings. Very tenderly he pointed out the positive aspects of the rare opportunity that we had been given. These people had come to us. They were eager to hear the Christian message. How could we fail them? We had been given a unique privilege. Deep down inside, I wanted to do my part. I made up my mind once and for all that I would stay. I began to count my blessings, trusted God to take care of our health, and kept on scratching. Finally, just before dawn I fell asleep.

The sun came up. A new day had dawned. I heard the sounds of people walking about outside, then a grinding noise. Women had already started their daily tasks, grinding the daily ration of wheat for bread. Someone was sweeping the dirt courtyard in front of each hut with a straw broom, stirring up dust with each sweep of the broom.

Nancy and I got up together. Domji's wife Mariam directed me towards the outside toilet. I had long dreaded this moment. The village women got up early, partly to relieve themselves in privacy away from the men folk. Their designated area was at the edge of the village, outside the stick fence encircling the village. I stood there, reluctant to move ahead.

Hu came to my rescue.

"You will never believe this," he said, directing me to a toilet.

Nancy and I headed outside the village and across the field, carrying a small roll of toilet paper. We were surprised and pleased at what we saw. A heavy straw mat, normally used to heighten the sides of an oxcart, had been rolled, spiral like, to form a privacy wall. It was about five feet high. Following the inside of the spiral, I saw a hole about two feet deep had been dug into the ground to form a latrine. Oh the joy of a privy!

—

By seven, we were served breakfast, tea and *chappaties*, a thin wheat bread cooked over an open fire.

Afterwards, we toured the village. Life was simple for the villagers. Some worked at hand looms. A tailor sat on the ground with his hand-operated sewing machine, stitching or mending garments. A few goats were around, the source of milk for the tea. Everyone was busy doing something useful such as shaking out bedding, hauling water from a nearby open well or gathering branches to be used as fuel for cooking.

I spent the morning chatting with the women. I sat on a short stool. The women squatted on their haunches. Nearly everything they did was in a squatting position. They would not allow me to do anything. Among themselves, the women referred to Nancy as a little princess. At one point, they ran their fingers through Nancy's hair, held an animated discussion and then said "no." Apparently, she didn't have lice. This act was a gesture of thoughtfulness and caring. They often checked each other's head for lice.

The village women laughed at my short hair. Even though my hair was shoulder length, it was still short to them. My ears at that time were not pierced and they could not understand why. I did not wear bracelets and that was also strange to them. The Marwari women, even the poorest, have pierced ears, earrings and a full set of bracelets around each wrist; almost always, they would have nose rings and wear heavy ankle bracelets as well. I explained that I did, indeed, have jewelry, but only wore it to special events such as a wedding.

The fact that I was wearing Pakistani clothes met with approval. One woman recalled seeing an English woman on the highway wearing a dress and her legs showed. They wondered if she were wearing short pants underneath. I assured them that she was wearing short pants underneath, though refraining from telling them just how short.

Most Mariwari women go through life with only two changes of clothes. One is the old one, worn every day. The other is a newer one. When the old one is completely worn out, she gets a new outfit.

A new outfit is a relatively costly expenditure, requiring some twelve yards for the skirt alone. The skirt is very full with a drawstring. Rather than drawing the string around the waist, it is drawn tightly below the navel and when she squats, the skirt folds naturally between the legs, appearing to look as if she is wearing full pantaloons. The blouse is tight-fitting and tied on the side, something like a wraparound and covers the bare midriff. A long, flowing, bright head covering also draping over the bosom completes the outfit. The entire outfit is colorful, made of bright reds, yellows, and greens. Taken together, the effect is quite stunning, making the tribal women stand out beautifully in the otherwise drab desert landscape.

Throughout our time in the village, the women got more and more personal with me. They did not wear undergarments. However, they wanted to know what I wore under my clothes. One woman tried to peer down my dress. I stopped her, knowing that if she succeeded others would surely follow. I wasn't quite ready to bare all.

They understood no English and I had never heard their own tribal language spoken before. Under the circumstances, we resorted to Sindhi as an imperfectly understood third language, common to both of us. When words failed, we resorted to sign language.

—

Later in the morning, as the sun rose higher, the early morning chill began to wear off.

"Would you like a bath?" I was asked.

Indeed, I very much wanted to bathe, but how would this work? Would I have to hide behind bushes to get a bath? I was mentally preparing myself to go the entire week without a bath. The village women did not bathe every day. We had spent the night in their home, under their covers. We had accepted their hospitality in every way. A family moved out of their hut to provide shelter for us. They slept outside in the open and the night air was cold. We were deeply moved by their generosity. However, in fairness to the family who had vacated their hut for us, we offered our unused tent for them to sleep in. "No," they said. It was cold at night and we were concerned about the family sleeping outside. Later, someone came up with a suggestion that we move into the tent ourselves and the family return to their hut.

Thankfully, the villagers themselves thought of this arrangement. We set up our tent, zipped up the front flap and decided that Nancy and I could bathe in the tent. Someone brought us a bucket of water. Nancy and I took turns standing just outside the tent for the other to get a bath. Out of view of the many villagers who seemed even more curious about our customs than we were of theirs, we managed a daily bath. I never saw a woman take a bath the entire week we were there.

Hu was not so fortunate. He had to learn how to bathe out near the open well just as the men did. He became familiar with a *dhoti*, a wide cotton cloth that wrapped around his waist. Nimbly, he held the cloth with one hand, bathing himself, undressing, and dressing inside the *dhoti* with the other, never exposing himself.

Lunch was served in the mid afternoon. Okra and tomatoes were in season and we ate them every day. Although I grew up in the American South, I had never liked okra. The women made delicious okra and I have loved it ever since.

While sharing in the life of the village, we maintained our practice of drinking boiled water, boiling it every day on the kerosene stove. We explained that our doctor required us to boil our drinking water.

Later in the week, a village man became quite ill with a high fever. We gave him aspirin, which did not help him. Someone suggested we give him some of our boiled water. They reasoned if boiled water kept us healthy, it should also have the power to heal the sick. We shared our boiled drinking water.

I watched with interest how the village women washed their dishes. First a woman took the dishes out into the yard and made a paste of dirt and water, rubbing it into the dishes, one dish at a time. She then took a bucket of cold water and rinsed them, placing them on a tray to dry. The water came from an open well. At mealtime, she took a multi-purpose cloth, wiped the dust off, and served her guests.

I observed a young mother as she prepared food with her small daughter beside her the entire time, nursing at her sagging breast. As far as I could tell, no one ever washed his/her hands. Our custom of washing hands before and after every meal must have seemed strange to them. In this village, soap and water were luxuries.

Every woman in the village remained busy throughout the day. One woman was mixing mud with straw to build a hut. Her young son mixed the mud with his feet while she mixed with her hands. In another part of the village, women were making large mud vessels to be used as storage bins for grain. Some of the women worked in the fields.

We visited a nearby village where the people did not even have mud huts, living instead under the trees. A woman in this village had just delivered a baby, a rope-strung bed served as a delivery table. Based on her complaints, I suspected she might have a post-partum infection. Medical facilities were far away.

Our hosts wanted us to visit other villages further away, requiring an overnight trip. I was dubious, although I knew the men all wanted to go. However, if I decided to go, there would not be enough room in the Land Rover for all of them. Reluctantly, I decided Nancy and I would stay behind. Hu and a dozen or more men piled into the Land Rover for the village some distance away.

We were miles off the highway with no electricity or telephone. The son of our host, Anthony, was assigned to look after Nancy and me. He followed us everywhere throughout the day and even into the night, maintaining a respectable distance from our tent.

I had brought Nancy's favorite doll along for her to have something familiar to play with. The doll proved to be a novel item, causing excitement wherever she went. News of the doll preceded us. In one home, a little girl became so attached to the doll that she cried when it was time for us to leave. It was a bad idea to bring the doll and later I managed to quietly withdraw it from circulation.

Nancy did not need the doll at all. She was excited about her freedom and made new discoveries every day. Our host's little girl, Martha, stuck with Nancy from the time we got up until we went to bed. I had no idea what they were doing,

"Guess what, mommy?" She excitedly announced to me at one point. "Today, I touched a cobra."

Indeed, a snake charmer lived at the edge of the village and he allowed the two little girls to see and touch the cobra that he kept in his basket.

———

After our week in the village, Martha often came with her father whenever he visited us in Shikarpur. Martha and Nancy had fun together. Once I filled two big metal tubs with water and let them play, giving each of them a bottle of soap bubble liquid to play with. Martha had never seen such magic and she was captivated by the flying bubbles. As she kept blowing, I kept refilling the bottle. She was not used to soap and water either and when she finally got out of the tub, her little body was wrinkled from the water.

When Nancy went away to boarding school, their meetings became much less frequent. However, Martha never forgot Nancy. Anytime we saw her she always asked about Nancy. Years passed and Nancy returned to America and college. She finished college and married. We wanted her husband Jeff to visit Pakistan where Nancy had grown up.

We helped them plan their trip so the two of them could together visit all the places where Nancy had lived. Shikarpur had been our home for most of Nancy's years in Pakistan. Martha had also grown up and married. She married at a much younger age than Nancy. Now Martha herself was living with her family in Shikarpur and she invited us into her home for tea. We had not seen Martha or her parents for many years. The reunion was poignant for all of us.

Married when she was about fourteen, Martha looked old for her age. She had several children. One little girl was about eight years old. Through the years, Martha had spoken of Nancy many times to her children. The little girl kept her eyes fixed on Nancy throughout our visit and she reminded me very much of Martha when she was a little girl.

After a while, Martha asked Nancy to come with her into the next room. Nancy complied. When they both emerged a few minutes later, Martha was smiling from ear to ear. Nancy followed her, wearing Martha's wedding finery.

This *Marwari* wedding dress was much different from those worn by Muslim and Christian women. It had two pieces—a full flowing skirt, tied with a drawstring and made from cotton print; and a tight-fitting bodice wrap around style and tied on the side. She also had a full bright scarf draped over her head and body. It was nearly the same as the one Martha was wearing except the embroidery and mirror work was more elaborate. Most likely she was keeping it for her daughter's wedding.

Martha's little girl looked at Nancy and then she looked at her mother.

"Mother, is this the Nancy you have always told me about?" She asked.

"Yes, this is Nancy," Martha replied.

It was hard for me to hold back the tears as I remembered the week we had spent in Martha's village nearly three decades before.

Chapter Twelve

FAMILY

Just a few months into our marriage, Hu and I sat before a group of serious-looking men in Chicago, board members of the mission organization that would send us to Pakistan. We were questioned about our theological beliefs and the motivations behind our desire to spend the rest of our lives in Pakistan. One man directed his question to me.

"Mrs. Addleton," he asked. "How do you feel about sending your children to a boarding school?"

I was speechless. We had no children. I had never ever thought about boarding school. Of course, we had hopes of children, but that was in the future. I answered him truthfully.

"I don't really know," I said. "But I will have to consider this when and if the time ever comes."

My answer must have been satisfactory as there were no further questions concerning the subject.

By the end of 1954 we were blessed with the birth of our first-born, David. The question of boarding school seemed mostly theoretical and was still some years away. Before it would become reality we added to our family—Jonathan in 1957 and Nancy in 1959. We were in the United States on leave when David started first grade at a local county school in Middle Georgia. His teacher, Berta Morton, was a wonderful woman. She was an effective teacher who had taught one of my younger sisters when she started first grade many years before.

When we returned to Pakistan for our second tour of ministry in 1961, David was entering second grade. The issue of boarding school was now a reality and we had to address it. All of his life David had heard about boarding from older children and he, not really knowing what was involved, looked forward to it as an adventure. So, without a whole lot of thought, we followed the lead of other parents who had been sending their children to boarding school for years.

I sewed name tags on every garment and every piece of linen and painted his name on other belongings. These were packed into a small metal foot locker that he took with him to the boarding school in Murree. He would spend the next ten years of his school life in a boarding school environment. Murree Christian School was about seven hundred miles from where we lived--two long days by road or about thirty hours by train. We hugged and then he left to join his friends, seemingly as happy as could be. Our feelings were mixed. In fact, the prospect of separation tore at our hearts. I was about ready to pack up and return to the United States.

Home schooling might have been an alternative, though the concept was much less practiced among the missionary community during the 1950's and 1960's than it is today. The only formal home school curriculum available was the Calvert course. Enrolling him in a local school was not a serious option. On the contrary, even middle-class Pakistanis routinely sought to have themselves transferred out of remote provincial towns such as Shikarpur for the sake of their children. They considered the local system of education to be inadequate.

With these circumstances in mind, we regarded placing him at Murree Christian School as our only option. He was away for three months at a time before we were able to see him again. We wrote either a card or a letter every day. I also prepared cookies and treats, always enough to share with his friends. As required by the school, he wrote to us at least once a week.

I kept every letter David wrote, as well as those subsequently written by his brother Jonathan and sister Nancy. The first ones were printed and short. They were filled with descriptions of the many activities school staff had prepared, including movie nights, hikes into the mountains and overnight camping along a river. All in all he seemed to be making a good adjustment. The teaching staff was addressed as "Mr." or "Ms."

while the boarding personnel were referred to as "Auntie" or "Uncle," endearing terms indicating a close family relationship. After all, they were surrogate mothers and fathers who loved and tenderly cared for our children. We both had bouts of loneliness without him and we yearned to see him. As the countdown began, I marked a calendar to keep me posted on the number of days before he would return home.

Jonathan went to kindergarten the following summer in preparation for boarding school. He was younger than David had been when he entered boarding and we could not leave him. I, therefore, made plans to teach him first grade. The school provided materials for me and I made a serious effort to become a teacher. However, it was not a good experience for either of us. I expected too much from him and often became impatient. It wasn't long before we both were ready for boarding school.

Following the winter break, he joined David on the long train ride from Sukkur to Rawalpindi through many stops in the Punjab, including Multan, Sahiwal, Lahore, Gujranwala and Jhelum. Hu accompanied them and there were other children and parents joining them on the long trip as they made their way to boarding. Once in Rawalpindi, the students and their chaperons boarded buses for the two hour trip through snow covered mountains to Murree.

Jonathan copied letters from the black board that his teacher had written for the class, just as David had done. When he began writing on his own, Jonathan was very expressive in his letters to us. He always asked about the people around us. He and David shared news about each other. While David was more reserved, Jonathan never hesitated to let us know if he felt homesick. Once he wrote a poem that was published in the school paper about being homesick. It was poignant and heart-felt:

"In bed when I lie, why should I cry?
Why should I be homesick when my parents aren't near?
Why should I shed a watery tear?
Just one and a half more months and I'll be there
In my parents' care."

In re-reading their letters as well as reading between the lines, I discovered that David did give us clues about his feelings and the fact he missed home. Often he would ask us to send small items he wanted.

Once, he wanted string and told us exactly where to find it in his room. As he grew older he shared more. We were deeply moved when he shared with us that he had a girl friend, his first. One week a letter came giving us her initials. The next week he gave us her name. He also told us about their first date.

When Nancy entered boarding school she devised a code to let us know when she was homesick. She drew a little house with a thermometer sticking out the doorway. She also wrote about seeing her brothers and news about them that perhaps they had not shared. During one boarding session, Jonathan had been quite ill and she wrote every day giving us a report. Nancy missed our poodle, Dixie. And she missed her cat Albert. We had numerous cats and they were hard to keep around. Albert was special. We know that Albert had nine lives because he had already used up so many of them. He was bright, had good habits and interacted well with children.

During vacation one winter, Nancy told us about the mice in her hostel. Her housemother, "Auntie Eunice," had been unsuccessful in getting rid of them. Nancy suggested a cat would help in keeping the mice away. She wanted to bring Albert to boarding. Of course the school had rules, one of which stated "no pets allowed." Nancy did not give up. Correspondence flew back and forth. It took special permission from the administration, but Albert was allowed to go to boarding to keep the mice away. I suggested to Nancy she should write a story, "When Albert the Cat Went to Boarding School."

During the long train ride north to school, Albert accompanied the children. Nancy prepared a bed in a basket for him. Albert slept most of the way. He went to boarding school—and the mice disappeared, just as Nancy said they would. Quite apart from his effectiveness in controlling rodents, Albert also became a much-loved figure in the hostel for many years to come.

———

Throughout the years, I always had mixed feelings regarding boarding and sending the children away for such a distance and for such a long period of time. The school was innovative in planning the year. Classes began in September and continued until December. It was winter in the mountains from December to March and often the roads to Murree were closed due to the heavy snowfall. For this reason, the school closed for the three winter months, when the weather in Sindh and Punjab was ideal. Following winter vacation, the children returned to school for the spring term followed by a three month summer term when it was particularly pleasant in the mountains. Mothers went to Murree during the summer months, escaping the severe heat on the plains. Living in small apartments or cottages on the hillside, mothers collected their children from boarding. For three months our children lived with me, attended classes during the day and returned home. The school bus picked them up and dropped them off daily. It was routine. It sounds complex but in reality our children were with us half the time.

When possible, we arranged ways to see them during their boarding terms. Domestic air travel entered our world and they could come home for long weekends. At other times, we managed to arrange an occasional trip to Murree to see them. It was often difficult but somehow we tried to be philosophical about it, making the most out of our peculiar arrangement. Many years later, Jonathan detailed his boarding experiences in *Some Far and Distant Place*, a memoir published by University of Georgia Press.

Once on home leave I talked to a good friend about my ambivalent feelings. As the children grew older, it was if anything becoming harder rather than easier to send them away to boarding school.

"At least you know where they are," she told me. "You can't say that about a lot of children today. Parents have no idea where their children are and what they are doing."

The educators and boarding parents at Murree Christian School felt a calling to their particular vocation. We appreciated their dedication and commitment. However, this did not insure that all was well all of the time. Serving briefly on the school board gave me insight into some of the problems, both large and small, the school faced. Some staff selected for the school did not work out. For older students, drugs at times became an issue. Drugs are widely available all over Pakistan. In fact, marijuana grew wild around the mountainside.

One positive feature about boarding school is that it helped the children learn responsibility at an early age. From the very beginning, this included practical lessons in making beds, tidying a room and getting along with others. They also learned to study independently. With no television to distract them, they learned to enjoy both reading and writing. They learned empathy and they learned to share, in part by sharing with their classmates the occasional care packages received from home. They learned to care, both for their classmates and in their interactions with the Pakistani housekeeping staff around them. These are only a few examples of some of the good aspects of boarding school life. To this day, our children continue to maintain strong relationships formed during their boarding school years in Pakistan.

——

What are some of the things I have learned on account of the boarding school experience from a parent's perspective? Perhaps most importantly, I learned I could not give my children all they needed as they developed into maturity. We sought to pass on to each of them the moral and spiritual values important to character development and which shaped our own lives. At the same time, our children needed other children as well as other adults. They also needed a wider social environment, one that was diverse, challenging, and reflected an ethos of service to others.

We had chosen a life of ministry that took us to Pakistan. We had felt a call and we believed that by following God's direction in fulfilling this call, spiritual resources would be available to us. True, our children were not born with a call, but they were born into our care as gifts from God. Along with these gifts came responsibility, a responsibility we accepted seriously. Without faith in God who directed our own lives we could not have adequately brought up our children in the unique life style that was ours.

I learned complete dependence on God. I believed God would keep our children safe, hundreds of miles from us. I trusted God to keep them healthy in the midst of disease and often unhealthy environments. I asked for God's help in providing good and strong surrogate parents. Some of them had flaws, just as we parents have flaws. I depended on God to enable our children to grow physically, mentally, and spiritually.

All three of our children are productive and happy adults. The road to maturity was not always smooth and along the way there were disappointments and heartache. Is not this true for everyone? All three graduated from college with honor and distinction. All three have earned post graduate degrees, mapped out professional careers, married and have children of their own.

David has an MA in philosophy and a JD, having qualified for the bar in both Illinois and Georgia. He has taught law, worked in general law practice, and provided legal services for members of a major auto workers union. Divorced after nineteen years of marriage, he is the father of two lovely daughters, Adriana and Alexandra. Besides his daughters, his passion is hiking the Appalachian Trail and hopes to complete the entire trail from Georgia to Maine some day. His interest in genealogy has helped our families discover interesting links to our past.

Jonathan earned his MA and PhD and has had a career with the State Department, serving with USAID in various countries including Pakistan, Cambodia, Jordan, South Africa, Yemen, Kazakhstan, and Mongolia. He married Fiona Riach from Scotland and they have three children, Iain, Cameron and Catriona, each born on a different continent.

Perhaps the highlight of Jonathan's career was the opportunity to return to Pakistan as country director for US assistance programs. One area of special responsibility focused on reconstruction following the massive earthquake in northern Pakistan in October 2005 that left nearly 80,000 dead and another 2.5 million homeless. During his tenure as USAID Mission Director in Pakistan, his official duties included opening a birthing station in Murree near where he was born and launching health and training programs in Upper Sindh not far from Shikarpur where he had grown up. At each event he delivered his remarks in Urdu and Sindhi. Recently, President Obama appointed him as U.S. Ambassador to Mongolia where he now serves.

Nancy earned her MA as well as RN and has had a career in hospital administration. She is married to Jeff White and they have one son, John. Recently, she became interested in local politics and was elected to the Macon City Council.

Running against a candidate who had been raised in Middle Georgia, the fact that Nancy had been born in Pakistan and spent her early years there briefly became a campaign issue. When asked by the media about the strength of her ties to Macon, she replied that it was true; she had been born in Pakistan—but all four of her grandparents are buried in Middle Georgia. When asked by a newspaper reporter if she had been raised to respect certain Southern values, even while growing up in South Asia, her reply was quick and to the point: "Well, for starters," she said, "My mother used carrots to make sweet potato pie."

We are proud of our children and their accomplishments and are blessed to have six grandchildren as an added source of joy and pleasure.

Chapter Thirteen

BEGINNINGS

The philosopher Soren Kierkegaard commented that life must be "lived forwards but understood backwards." The poet T.S. Eliot wrote that "the end of all our exploring will be to arrive where we started and know the place for the first time." In the autumn of my life, I can appreciate the truth of those statements. After more than three decades in Pakistan, I returned to Middle Georgia where I was born and raised. Looking back, I see a pattern and purpose in my life. Memories from the thirty-four years that I have spent in Pakistan figure prominently in my musings. But memories of Middle Georgia, where life for me began, also loom large. It was that early childhood and adolescence that gave shape to the person I have become.

Until I was eleven, my life was idyllic. As a middle child in a family of eight, responsibilities came early. My older sister Sara made sure that I took on as many of hers as she could pass on to me. As in rural Pakistan, it was always understood the older siblings would take care of the younger ones. Large families such as ours had built-in baby sitters. As my older sister cared for me, in turn, I was expected to care for the younger ones. My two older brothers, Raymond and James were exempt from child-caring. They were given outside chores.

There were four younger sisters, Jennell, Shirley, Josephine, and Mary Frances, all born within two years or less of each other. Growing up together we were all close and got along well. We had great fun. We shared everything. When my brother got a bicycle, it was understood that any of us could ride the bike, although technically it belonged to him.

My little sister Jennell and I loved to play "house." We would define an area outside under the shade of a china berry tree, mark it off with stones or branches and divide it into rooms. We used tree branches to make a broom and kept our "house" very clean. Our dolls and tea sets made playing seem realistic. My great aunt Agnes, an Italian, gave me a new china tea set for Christmas every year. Once we found some bricks and made ourselves a stove. Searching for empty tin cans we turned them into pots and pans. Mama wasn't too happy when we built a fire in our brick stove and tried to cook.

Sometimes Mama left us alone with big sister in charge. She always left chores for us because she believed firmly that "idle minds and hands are the devil's workshop." There were bushels of peas or butter beans to shell and endless cleaning up needing to be done. Almost always, there was also a little one to tend who would wind up being a real live baby in our make-believe game of playing house.

We must have been poor but didn't realize it at the time. I was born in 1931, just when the Great Depression was reaching its deepest point. My parents had moved from South Georgia to Jones County in Middle Georgia, not far from Macon. Times were difficult for rural folk.

"We were doing all right until Bettie came along," I heard my mother say at one point. "She was a big surprise."

My father had an uncle whom we all considered rich. He was a business man. He owned land. We lived on his farm. When my parents moved to the farm, my uncle's sister and her husband lived there and they occupied the big house. We lived in the smaller tenant house. That was my first home, the place where I was born. I have the distinction of being the first in my family to have had a medical doctor in attendance.

All of us were born at home. After my birth in the tenant house, four others came along. A local woman attended at each birth as a sort of midwife. I vaguely remember when one of my younger sisters was born. I was packed off along with my other sisters to the midwife's house for overnight and her older daughters helped care for us. When we returned to our own home the next day, we were met with the cries of a new baby.

In those years, women stayed in bed for at least a week following child birth. Looking back, it was very probably the only time for rest they ever had. A young Negro woman called Dottie always came to help care for Mama and the newborn.

Once when one of my younger sisters was born I was not "packed off" and remained at home in the next room. During the night, I was awakened by muffled talking. "Well, the doctor can just put her in his little black bag and take her back to where she came from," my mother was exclaiming, having just been told that she had given birth to yet another daughter.

With only two older boys followed by a several girls, I'm sure my parents must have been disappointed. Still, we all felt loved and very much a family.

One day my aunt and uncle and some cousins who lived in the "big house" moved away. We missed them, but, with their departure, we moved into the larger house. In reality, the "big house" consisted of only two bedrooms, a living room, a kitchen and an outhouse. As we sometimes commented, for all practical purpose our home was simply "four rooms and a path".

Other relatives moved into the small house we had vacated. We had everything we needed: cows, goats, pigs, chickens, fruit trees and vegetable gardens.

One year we even grew cotton. Every available hand was enlisted to pick it. I was not old enough to pick the cotton but I was old enough to watch the small children. When the cotton picking season was over I was allowed to choose a dress from the Sears Roebuck Catalog as compensation for my efforts. The dress was white organdy with a sailor collar. This dress was a special reward because I usually wore hand-me-downs passed on by my city cousins—either that, or dresses sewn up from printed feed sacks.

One of my regular chores was churning butter in a tall earthenware churn with a wooden paddle on the end of a long stick. Remarkably, this was very similar to the clay churns I later saw in the villages of rural Pakistan.

When I operated a butter churn as a child, I got sleepy. I often sang to try and stay awake. One of the songs that helped keep me awake went like this:

"Come butter come;
Come butter come;
Johnny's at the garden gate,
Waiting for a butter cake;
Come butter come."

Mama had a pretty wooden butter mold. When the butter finally made, she cooled it and molded it into lovely shapes. We also used the fresh buttermilk to drink as well as for baking.

During the summer harvest season, we all picked and shelled peas and butter beans. We also picked vine-ripened tomatoes from our kitchen garden. Mama spent hours canning vegetables. Sometimes she turned them into soup. Every conceivable type of berry was used to make jams and jellies. We also dried apples and peaches, placing them on the tin roofs of our house and barn. Our outdoor smoke house was lined with shelves and Mama filled every space with her harvest.

I found farm work very boring. But I loved some parts of it, including making home made ice cream using fresh cream, whole milk and farm fresh eggs. When the peaches were ripe, we made fresh peach ice cream. At other times, we picked blackberries and added them into the mixture.

My dad worked in Macon, not on the farm. It was my mother who operated the farm, milking cows, tending the other animals, running the house and cooking for the family and the many relatives who visited now and then. She also sewed clothes for us. In the evening, she crocheted. I wish I still had the beautiful bedspread she crocheted when I was a little girl.

Mama managed the farm but she also had help. Cousins who had moved on to the farm helped as did my brothers, older sister and the rest of us. For some reason, my brothers especially loved the goats. They hitched the goats up to a wagon and we lined up for rides down the hill, dangerous but fun and excitement.

My assigned job at one point was to feed the chickens and gather the eggs. I dreaded collecting the eggs because I had once met a long black snake trying to get at the eggs ahead of me. From then on, I became deathly afraid of snakes.

—

I started school at the age of five. It was an adventure from the first day. After a big breakfast, my siblings and I walked about a half mile to catch the bus. It arrived early in the morning because it picked up children all along the route, and ours was one of the first stops.

We carried our lunches with us. Usually, lunch consisted of a single piece of ham or thick bacon, often covered with cane syrup and wrapped in a large biscuit from the breakfast batch. Because we got picked up early, we were among the first to be dropped off at the end of the day. Mama always had something ready for us to eat when we returned home from school. My favorite snack was bread pudding which could be sliced easily when eaten cold. It was delicious with a glass of milk. Supper in the evening was a large spread. My dad expected meat and fresh biscuits at every meal and my mother never disappointed him.

My parents did not attend church. Annually, a visiting preacher came around and services were held in various homes in the community. My parents attended these meetings and sometimes fed the preachers.

Two women in the community, Mrs. Frances and Mrs. Mary, took special interest in the spiritual welfare of the children who lived in our corner of Jones County. They gathered those of us who wanted to come for Bible lessons and songs in an old one-room school house. I loved being part of the "Sunbeam Band." The women told exciting stories of missionaries in very faraway places. One story was about a missionary woman named Lottie Moon who served the people of China. I had no idea where China was but from that time on I had a desire to go to some far and distant place. I must have passed this desire on to my children who are also well traveled. Indeed, when my son Jonathan wrote his own memories of growing up in Pakistan, he used this line as the title for his book, calling it *Some Far and Distant Place.*

Each summer, the two women encouraged us to attend Vacation Bible School at First Baptist Church in Gray, a small town about seven miles away. I was able to ride with them into Gray. It was difficult for Mama to let me go at such a busy time of year, but she did. I loved every one of the activities.

This lovely little world had cracks through which I sometimes peeped. As I mentioned, my father did not work on the farm. He was the butcher in my uncle's store, the Broadway Super Market in Macon, about ten miles away. The farm supplied the store with fresh vegetables, eggs, chickens, and milk products.

Not all of my uncle's business ventures were legal. Although national prohibition had by this time ended, many counties across Georgia were still dry. Jones County was one of them. I was a child and don't remember all the details. But I vividly recall the aura of mystery surrounding much of what he did. I also remember that my own father was frequently out of town. We were told that he was transporting dishes from up north. At night, I was sometimes awakened by the sound of rattling glass. Of course, I figured these were the dishes my parents talked about. In fact, there were some dishes—these had been placed on top of contraband liquor.

I don't know how long the farm was used as a storage and transit point for whiskey. However, I do know that one day everything changed. My uncle sold the farm and my family moved to Macon. My mother cried as I had never seen her cry before.

We moved into a large house in a pleasant neighborhood. We also transferred from Jones County to Bibb County schools. Some of my memories from this time are vague. However, I do recall that the best grade we could get on our report card was a "G" for good. If we made all "G's," we went to the nearby Chichester's Drug Store at Tattnall Square for a free ice cream. I managed to get an ice cream every time I got a report card.

The move to Macon marked the beginning of a dark period for the family. My dad began to drink too much, and he found it difficult to get a job or to keep one. My mother was very unhappy because she loved living in the country and wanted a garden.

Despite the difficulties facing my parents, I loved my new school and had many friends in the neighborhood. Once we set up a small stage and performed for anyone we could persuade to come and watch us. I also attended a little church nearby. The service was very emotional and loud and I never really felt part of the congregation.

Later, we moved about halfway between Macon and Gray, near US
129, the main highway connecting Bibb County with Jones County.
From the beginning, I was ashamed to live in that house. It was a
wooden, unpainted structure with four rooms and a large porch. The
kitchen was detached from the main house but connected by a covered
passageway. Later, this outside kitchen was torn down and my mother
used the living room as a kitchen as well as a living and dining room.
Down a well-trodden path was our outhouse, perhaps another source
of my embarrassment.

We drew water from an outside well in the yard to the side of the
house. On days my mother washed clothes, we children had to draw
the water, using a rope and a bucket. We took turns drawing the water,
bucket by bucket, filling the wash tubs. If it wasn't done before going
to school, we had to stay home to do it. I never wanted to miss school
and tried to make sure this chore was always done on time.

Our house had a large yard surrounded by woods. I especially loved
the crabapple trees and their beautiful blossoms. My sisters and I often
played underneath those trees, which neatly formed a canopy over us.
My brother once built a tree house. He allowed us to play in it until I
suggested hanging some curtains. Another fun activity was near a small
stream. We had discovered white clay along the banks and took great
pleasure in molding various items and placing them in the sun to dry.
Curiously, we made cooking pots and pans or other items related to
the house. I never thought of creating statues or abstracts. My brother
discovered a very strong vine which we enjoyed swinging from and we
often swung from one side of the creek to the other. Once we cut down
some small trees, notched them, and attempted to build a log cabin.
We never got very far in this project. Although poor by the standards of
some, we were happy in the world we had created for ourselves.

The move to the unpainted house near the US Highway 129
brought many changes, beginning when my older brother Raymond
left to join the army in World War II. We sadly waved goodbye as he
walked down the dirt road to the nearby highway where he caught
a bus to Fort McPherson in Atlanta for his induction. I wrote him
faithfully when he was shipped off to East Asia to take part in the war

against Japan. He sent photos and we always prayed for his safety. My other brother James lied about his age and joined up, too, though the war ended before he could be sent overseas.

Perhaps the biggest change occurred when my mother, who had never worked outside the home in her entire life, joined the hordes of other women working in ordinance factories. My dad worked as a carpenter and builder, though he found work only sporadically. Financially, these were hard times for us.

My older sister Sara found a job as a waitress in a nearby barbecue restaurant. With her departure, I took over more household chores. A neighbor with an infant son called on me to help her care for him. Her home was probably a mile from our home and I had to walk. I don't remember getting paid for this but I did receive small gifts for my hope chest including pillow cases made from feed sacks. I learned to embroider flowers and butterflies on them to make them more beautiful. I ended up giving them to Sara when she married.

My sister Sara walked to her job at the restaurant. She was not allowed to walk on the highway alone. Usually, two of the younger sisters accompanied her. It was fun in the summer but it was often sunny and hot.

One day, I had just returned from my baby-sitting job when Sara was ready to go to work. She had been waiting for me to come so that she could leave. Naturally, I was tired and said I did not want to go. In fact, I resisted fiercely and made excuses to keep from going. It was not a pleasant scene. In the end, two younger sisters went in my place. I was eleven years old and they were eight and ten. The two sisters, Jennell and Shirley, walked Sara to her job and were returning home along the highway. Not long after the time they should have been returning home, a Negro neighbor came screaming to our house, calling for my mother.

"There has been an accident," she shouted to us. "Jennell has been hit by a truck."

We were devastated. The sister who was with her was nearly hysterical with fear and horror at what had happened. My mother was driven immediately to the Macon Hospital where Jennell had been taken. Those of us at home waited long hours before receiving the news that her condition was grave. Jennell had suffered multiple brain injuries. Within twenty-four hours she was dead.

While relatives were informed and funeral arrangements set in place, I stood on the sidelines grieving my heart out. I should have been the one on the road that day. Had I gone she would not have been hit by a large wrecker truck, whose driver had momentarily taken his eyes off the narrow road. My two younger sisters had been holding hands as they walked. Tightly clutching each other's hands, the impact snatched them apart. When Jennell died, her little hand was curled in that clutching position. She was buried that way. Her lifeless body lay in a casket, her injuries wrapped in bandages.

Neighbors and friends from near and far mourned with us in this tragic loss. The funeral service was held in the high school auditorium in Gray. The funeral service did not end my grief. I could not sleep. Whenever I finally slept, I dreamed and always my dream was about someone getting killed. I would awaken from sleep, reliving the nightmare. Whenever a family member left, I worried incessantly about their safe return. It took years for me to put this tragic accident into perspective.

———

Whenever possible, I went to church with a neighbor, a spinster woman who picked me up on her way to the Baptist church in Gray. A Sunday school teacher took a personal interest in me. Once she planned a wiener roast for her class of teenaged girls. Of course, it was impossible for me to attend because I didn't live in town. When my Sunday school teacher found out that I was unable to attend, she came up with a wonderful solution. She asked me to stay after school, attend the wiener roast, spend the night with her and catch the school bus the next day. Sensing my joy, Mama gave me permission.

Arriving with my teacher at her home, I was overwhelmed. She showed me to her college daughter's room which was to be mine for the night. I had seen beautiful rooms in magazines, and here was a canopied bed with a bedspread of ruffles all the way to the floor. There was also a lovely dressing table with a lamp. The bed was high and I had to climb to get into it. The next morning, after a hearty breakfast, I was given a sack lunch, unlike those I took from my own home.

This lunch had sandwiches made with white bread and pimento cheese between the slices. I have never forgotten this special experience. I felt so important, so loved and accepted.

School functions that took place during the school hours were the only social outlet for me. Prom time when I graduated from seventh grade into high school presented special obstacles. I could not afford a long dress and transportation would be difficult. There was no way I could attend this event. When a classmate offered to lend me an evening dress I couldn't believe my luck. I went to the prom in a beautiful long blue ruffled evening gown. I cannot remember how I got there.

At the prom, each girl was given a little book and a pencil. As boys came around asking for a promenade his name was written in the little book beside a number. I was afraid I wouldn't be asked, but I was. Each prom lasted about five minutes. Couples walked around outside along a designated path, sometimes holding hands. In the semi-darkness, some couples managed to get even closer. I strolled with a handsome young man. As we turned the corner he said to me, "let's stand over here," guiding me to a semi-dark and secluded area. Before I knew what was happening, he managed to plant a kiss on my cheek. I was horrified at once and excited at the same time. This was my first kiss.

After about five proms, each with a different boy, there was an intermission. Refreshments were served, and the girls gathered in groups, giggling and exchanging reports of who their various escorts had been. I found out others had also been kissed while on these promenades. I couldn't help but wonder if the same boy who had kissed me also kissed every other girl that evening as he escorted them along the garden path.

About this time I began to keep a diary. I recorded everything I could think of. Because the little book had a key, I wanted to record everything, thinking it would be safely locked away. A tall good looking boy in school often smiled at me. I was pleased with his attention and experienced my first crush. I wrote in my diary words that I still remember: "Nobody knows it but I like Johnny."

This was my secret and mine alone. I did not take into account a mischievous brother who wanted to get his hands on my diary, and he did. One evening he danced around the house singing, "Everybody knows that Bettie loves Johnny." I was angry and crushed. I ripped the diary to shreds and threw it away. Since then I have been reluctant to divulge my inner secrets on the written page.

About this time a most interesting family moved nearby. Wilma, a girl my age, introduced herself to me at school and we became good friends. We rode the same school bus. She had a bicycle and used to cycle over to my house. In fact, she allowed me to learn to ride her bike. One evening, long after dark, I rode and rode around the house with her cheering me on until I got the knack of riding.

Wilma had older sisters who were worldly, and they passed on numerous facts of life that I had never learned. Sometimes she invited me to go to the movies with her family in Macon. She also passed along paperback novels for me to read which were considered trash by my values. Nevertheless, I read some of the books, especially those written by author Erskine Caldwell who made a career out of his descriptions of the seamier side of life in rural Georgia.

My friend had a camera which she loved to use. Once, in mid-winter, we got swim suits belonging to her sisters and put them on with a warm coat covering us. We walked down to a nearby lake. Each of us posed pin-up style and photographed each other. I don't really know what we were thinking but perhaps we expected to be discovered, whisked off to Hollywood and become famous.

Wilma also took me on a trip to Atlanta for a visit with her married sister. We hopped on a Greyhound bus, enjoying every moment. I had never been to Atlanta before. She had the experience and I admired her ability to take care of us. Upon arriving at the bus station in Atlanta she hailed a taxi. We rode around quite a few miles before finding the house. It was in Buckhead but the driver didn't seem to know where Buckhead was. I enjoyed the excursion into the big city. Other than to visit my grandmother in Jesup, I had never traveled very much.

Another aspect of life at that time was the relationship we had with our Negro neighbors across the creek behind our house. There were two older couples and we called the women "Aunt." Both couples had grown children who had married and left home. Periodically, they came with their children for a short visit. They never stayed very long. The sons were in the military, serving in the war, and they were proud of them. They also provided a regular income for their aging parents back in Georgia.

From time to time one or the other of the women was hired to stay with us when Mama was away. We called them Aunt Ida and Aunt Hattie. I especially loved Aunt Ida. She was a lot of fun and played along with our jokes. We sat on her lap and teased her. Once we shook the salt shaker on her head without her knowing and told her she had little white things in her hair. She had grey hair but the salt was detectable. We got a mirror to show her. Indeed, we had her scared that she might really have lice. Lovingly, she scolded us.

I visited Aunt Ida every chance I got. Although we were told never to eat at the homes of these precious women, I absolutely could not get enough of Aunt Ida's sweet potato pie. I would go there and without shame ask if she had any pie. She always responded, "Lawd, Miss Bettie, you know you ain't spose to eat my pie." All the time she was talking, she was on her way to her kitchen to cut me a slice of the most delicious pie I'd ever eaten.

Aunt Ida had three rooms and a large porch. One room was a big kitchen with a wood-burning iron stove. The dining room table was also there. The second was the living room with two iron beds, a dresser and some comfortable chairs. A wood-burning fireplace kept the room warm and cozy in winter. The walls were papered with newsprint which I am sure was for insulation. A single light bulb hung from the ceiling, providing the only illumination. An assortment of pictures hung on the wall and always there was an illustrated calendar.

The third room door was kept closed. That room had a matching bedroom set and pretty curtains hung at the windows. Picture frames of children and grandchildren adorned every available space. This room was kept for company and more probably for the children when they visited. It was my favorite room, and I begged Aunt Ida to allow me to change the furniture around and she did. Perhaps I was a budding interior decorator. At the very least, I had an interest, one that continued throughout my life in Pakistan where I worked to turn even the lowliest of sun baked brick houses in which we lived into a home.

I loved Aunt Ida and Aunt Hattie as much as I loved my own blood aunts. Aunt Ida was present when my youngest sister was born. The doctor had been summoned but did not arrive in time so Aunt Ida was called. She was our nearest neighbor.

Life was simple and it was also hard. There was hardly ever enough money for anything extra. I hated the Christmas holiday when we drew names and exchanged gifts at school. I always received a much nicer gift than I ever gave. Somehow we managed.

One morning, after breakfast, I caught my dad's attention and asked him when I could get new shoes. He told me he now had another job and I should be able to get some new shoes very soon. I was elated as I departed for school that day, full of optimism as I started planning for those new shoes.

The last school bell sounded in the afternoon and we all piled out of the building, going to our respective buses. I noticed the drivers had gathered in a circle, strained looks showing on their faces. This is what I heard them say: "There are reports a man has been killed on the highway. This is bad news. They don't yet know who it is."

My heart began pounding when I heard the drivers talking furtively among themselves in this way. I found my seat on the bus, still shaking from what I had just heard.

"Dear God," I said, whispering a prayer. "Please don't let it be daddy."

I was subdued all the way home. Usually, I was laughing on the school bus, having fun with my friends, but I was disturbed by what I had heard.

There was a hill above our house. As the bus reached the top of the hill, I looked down toward our house and saw a large number of cars parked on the roadside as well as in the yard. As the bus stopped in front of the house, my sister ran out to meet us.

"You don't need to tell me," I said to her, before she even had a chance to say a word, "I already know."

It was my dad who had been killed on the highway. He was on his way home from Macon and riding on the back of a truck. It stopped suddenly and he fell, hitting the pavement. We were told he died instantly.

The same Negro woman who brought the news of my sister's fatal accident had come to break this stunning news to my mother. I was crushed. Once again, relatives came from all over and joined friends and neighbors to mourn with us. My school friends came but I was inconsolable. We were all taken to the funeral home to view the body after it had been prepared. I still found it hard to believe.

The funeral was held at the First Baptist Church in Gray. I was unable to deal with my grief. Without being told, I knew this event would be life-changing for all of us. My mother, around 40 years old, still young and attractive, was left a widow with four young girls. My older sister had married; my older brother had finished his military tour; my other brother had migrated to Michigan to seek his fortune in the auto industry.

For a while, we stayed in our house near the Gray Highway. It must have been more than a year because I remember my mother had a suitor. He came in his nice automobile one evening and announced he was taking us to Macon to see the Christmas lights. I hated the sight of him. Reluctantly, I crawled into the back seat and pouted all the way. I refused the refreshments he offered to buy us. I don't remember him ever coming around again. A young widowed mother with four girls and one of them insolent probably scared him away.

My mother decided to use the insurance money from my father's death to buy a house and relocate to Macon. In retrospect, the decision was probably based on the idea that we young girls would have better opportunities in the city. It also meant that my mother would once again go to work.

The house my mother bought had three bedrooms along with a bathroom, living room, dining room and small kitchen. It also had a small front porch and a large yard, giving my mother plenty of room for flowers and whatever else she wanted to grow. It was located on a quiet street in a nice neighborhood about two blocks from the city bus line. That was important as we had no other transportation.

The house was brand new, just a square little box made of green asbestos shingles. The walls inside were covered with beautiful wall paper. We moved in and settled down quickly. My mother went to work at the Happ pants factory. I was fifteen, a junior in high school. When I arrived home from my new school, my younger sisters were already at the house. As the oldest still living at home, my job was to see that they behaved and finished their homework. I also prepared supper, making sure that it was always ready by the time my mother herself returned from work.

Money was tight, even with a Social Security check we received as minors plus my mother's wages. I got a job on Saturdays in a five and dime store downtown. I also worked as a baby sitter nearly every Friday and Saturday night. I was a country girl living in the city and I did not feel at home. The large school for girls that I attended was full of cliques and sororities. I never felt as if I belonged. In addition, for the first time in my school life I lacked enthusiasm for my studies. I pursued a course preparing me for employment once I graduated. In my senior year, I wrote off for college catalogues, knowing fully I would never be able to go. After all, I was the first child in my family to graduate from high school. What more could I ask?

While still in high school, I met some very nice girls who laughed and seemingly enjoyed each other. They were always talking about the fun they had and also about boys and their dates. I had none of that in my life. A young senior, I had just turned sixteen.

Although I had sometimes attended the Baptist church in Gray when we lived in the country, we were not a church-going family. Now that we had moved to Macon, I decided I wanted to find a church.

One bright Sunday morning, I walked two blocks to the bus line. Buses ran infrequently on Sundays so I had to wait a while. The first bus that came along went south, and I decided to hop on. I was pleasantly surprised to find others, all strangers, on the bus and dressed in Sunday clothes. We passed a couple of churches and no one got off. Further down the street, the bus stopped and nearly everyone got off. I did not see a church, but I got off with the crowd. They crossed the street and I crossed the street with them. A block away I saw a sign: "Mikado Baptist Church."

My discovery of this church turned out to be "the first day of the rest of my life." I was surprised to see some of the girls I had met in school were there. I was not a complete stranger after all. They were friendly and I immediately felt a welcomed part of this community. A few months later, I got up enough courage to go before the church and ask to become a member.

The pastor wanted to be sure that I understood what I was doing. He spent a long time showing me the Scriptures. I realized I needed and wanted an inner transformation, not just to join the congregation to meet my social needs. From that day, I began to study the Bible seriously. I attended every organization in the church I could. I wanted to learn everything possible about the Christian life. My life had changed and I had changed.

Following high school graduation, I went to work as was expected of me. My first job was with the telephone company. A few of my friends had gotten jobs there. It paid well and I enjoyed it. Also, it meant, with my income, it was easier for my mother to make ends meet. All was well until the job began to interfere with my church activities. I didn't want to miss a single event. It was difficult to inform my mother I was leaving a good job for a lower paying job as a bookkeeper in a flower shop. The new job allowed me to work nine to five, five days a week. Thus, I was free to fully participate in the life of the church.

Sometimes things are seldom what they seem to be and in due time I found out my services were needed in the flower shop for more than bookkeeping. My woman boss wanted to teach me how to design floral arrangements. She even mentioned sending me off for formal training as a designer. I was elated and found I had an interest. It gave me a creative outlet. As I learned more about the business, I was also given more responsibility. Much to my dismay, special holidays such as Mother's Day, Easter, weddings and other occasions often demanded my time on Sunday. Once again, conflicts between work and church life surfaced. I began searching for a new job.

The third try as a clerk in an insurance company seemed perfect. Finally, I had a real nine to five job, five days a week with no overtime and no Sunday work. It also offered opportunity for advancement as I briefly contemplated a career in the insurance world. I was earning well. I could afford shoes and clothes and even give more financial assistance to my mother in running the house. For a poor country girl, I had it made. I had friends, both male and female. I had plenty of time for church activities. What else was there in life?

My continued commitment to church brought challenges of another kind. Special speakers and missionaries came and presented their works and concerns. They came from every country imaginable. As I studied the Bible more seriously, I found out that God had a plan for my life and I wanted to respond to whatever His plan might be.

Therefore, again I wrote away for college catalogues, this time to Bible colleges and training schools to enlighten me on the future course of my life.

Still, it was almost impossible to conceive of an unknown future as a missionary, living a life perhaps fraught with hardships and loneliness. Besides, I wanted to get married. I wanted a husband and a family. Should I end up in some foreign land, this dream would in all probability be unrealized. Also, I had three younger sisters who still needed to get through school. Even with my mother's factory job, dress making and alteration jobs, her income was hardly enough for the increasing needs.

Conflicts inevitably arose within and without. With strong conviction, I declared publicly God's leading me into a life of full-time Christian service. If I followed this direction, I would need to go to Bible college. In spite of increasing difficulties I wanted to do everything possible in order to follow God's plan for my life as I felt it to be. My mother was terribly upset. My friends encouraged me. God's love and grace sustained me.

As the months went by, I felt the urgency to make the decision to leave my job which I loved and enroll in a Bible college. I believed in miracles. I never had much money but everything I needed, I had. I firmly believed that God would supply every need for me to strike out on the journey ahead. And so, I went to Tennessee Temple Bible College in Chattanooga. I worked many jobs—in the library, in a snack shop, in a lady's store, baby sitting for faculty members. My grades were good. In addition, I taught Sunday school, sang in the choir and became involved in outreach ministry.

I also had a social life although I was very careful in this aspect. Because I was planning a missionary career, I was reluctant to involve myself with anyone who did not share that dream. The determination to focus on God's plan gave me enormous freedom.

In what I consider perfect timing, I became re-acquainted with Hu, now a handsome young man whom I had known when he was a boy growing up in Jones County. His sister had been my best friend. At some point, our paths had gone in different directions. He had attended Columbia Bible College in South Carolina and was in seminary preparing for a life of missionary work. When, once again our paths crossed, we discovered to our utter amazement that, although we had taken a different journey, we had prepared ourselves for a common ministry.

I believe our marriage was made in heaven. I believe God took us from similar backgrounds, living just a few miles apart, and developed our character and potential. When we came together, we embodied the essence of what God's plan was for us. In all the years that we have been together, including the thirty-four years that we shared in Pakistan, we have never looked back. The uncharted future we chose to follow was the Divine fulfillment and perfect plan God had for us. What an incredible journey it has been!

GLOSSARY

Allah: God

Azaan: A call to prayer

Basmati: Long grain fragrant rice

Bearer: Servant whose job is serving the table and other personal jobs

Betel nut: The seed of the betel plant, a vine

Bihishti: A water carrier

Beyti: Daughter

Biryiani: Spicy rice mixed with vegetables or meat

Bismullah: Blessing

Bister: Bed roll used when traveling

Burra Din Mubarak: Blessings on the big day, referring to Christmas

Burka: Outer garment worn by women that covers from head to toe

Bustie: Ghetto

Cantonment: Military area where mostly Europeans lived during British era

Chappati: Flat bread cooked over open fire

Charpai: A rope-strung bed

Chit: Written notes of recommendation

Coolies: Laborers, carriers of baggage

Dai: Mid-wife

Dhoti: Garment worn by men; a wrap-around

Dhurrie: A rug

Dolie: A cabinet with screen wire to keep perishable items

Duputta: Head scarf worn by women

Eid: Religious holiday

Hazri: Tea served in bed before breakfast

Hookah: A water pipe

Khameez: Loose fitting tunic worn by women

Khuda Ka Shukkur: Thank God

Kinu: A citrus fruit similar to a tangerine

Mai: Respectful term for a woman

Majilis: A religious gathering

Mecca: Holy City for Muslims, in Arabia

Memsahib: Proper title when addressing a white woman

Mendhi: Henna

Muhajir: Refugee

Naan: Flat bread made with leavening

Otak: Reception room for meeting male guests

Paan: The green leaf of the betel plant

Pagal Khana: The name given to a Mental Hospital, meaning crazy
house

Paisa: Monetary unit, less than a cent, also general term for money

Pakora: Deep fried batter covered vegetable or meat snack

Punjabi Psalter: Psalms in the Punjabi language set to music

Quran: Holy Book for Muslims

Ramadan: Muslim month of fasting

Rat-Ki-Rani: A vine with a small white flower and a sweet smell, meaning "Queen of the Night"

Roshandan: A transom, high up on a wall to access light and cool breezes

Sahib: A polite term used in addressing a male

Samosas: A meat or vegetable patty encrusted with flaky dough, either fried or baked

Seekh Kabobs: Chunks of meat roasted on a skewer over fire

Seer: Unit of weight measure, about two pounds

Serai: An inn, used by camel caravans in ancient times

Shalwar: Full baggy pants on a drawstring, worn by both men and women

Shami Kabobs: Ground meat patties, fried

Tonga: One-horse carriage

Valima: Post wedding dinner, hosted by the groom's family

Zenana: Woman's exclusive domain